Leading with Hope, Faith, and Love

The Diane E. Randall Collection

First edition, March 2022
Published by the FCNL Education Fund

FCNL Education Fund
245 Second Street NE
Washington, DC 20002
800-630-1330
www.fcnl.org

Diane Randall, **Fourth General Secretary (2010–2021)**

Adlai Amor, **Managing Editor**
Kristen Archer, Alicia McBride, and Eric Bond, **Editors**
Wesley Wolfbear Pinkham, **Designer**

This work is licensed used the Creative Commons Attribution-NonCommercial 4.0 International License.

ISBN 978-1-7373704-1-3

Printed using vegetable inks on FSC®-certified paper in a facility powered by renewable energy.

*"Now faith, hope and love abide,
but the greatest of these is love."*

— 1 Corinthians 13:13

Table of Contents

8 **Foreword: Leading Hope and Building Trust**
by Marge Abbott

11 **Essay: Growth Anchored in Faith**
by Adlai Amor

22 **Powerful Beyond Measure: Trusting the Call to Leadership, Exercising Our Citizenship**
Philadelphia Yearly Meeting
July 28, 2011 » Philadelphia, PA

34 **Inspired Faith: Action in a Time of Conflict**
FCNL 2011 Annual Meeting
November 8, 2011 » Washington, DC

46 **Faith and Public Action**
William Penn University
September 18, 2012 » Oskaloosa, IA

56 **Power from Knowing God**
Congressional Prayer Breakfast of the
Churches for Middle East Peace
May 21, 2013 » Washington, DC

62 **The Future of Quaker Advocacy**
FCNL 2013 Annual Meeting
November 15, 2013 » Washington, DC

68 **Reimagining U.S. Foreign Policy**
Intermountain Yearly Meeting
June 12, 2014 » Ghost Ranch, NM

77 **Perfect Love Casts Out Fear**
Jamestown Friends Meeting
November 2, 2014 » Jamestown, NC

84 **A Multitude of Troubles**
FCNL 2015 Annual Meeting
November 12, 2015 » Washington, DC

95 **What We Need Is Here**
Dwight and Ardis Michener Lecture
Southeastern Yearly Meeting
January 17, 2016 » Orlando, FL

120 **From Despair to Strength and Joy**
North Pacific Yearly Meeting
July 14, 2016 » Spokane, WA

138 Spirit-Led Social Action
Stephen G. Carey Memorial Lecture
Baltimore Yearly Meeting
October 13, 2016 » Frostburg, MD

150 Healing the Heart of Democracy
FCNL 2016 Annual Meeting
November 11, 2016
Washington, DC

158 Standing in the Light: Power, Politics, and Prophecy
FCNL 2017 Annual Meeting
November 5, 2017
Washington, DC

178 FCNL at 75!
West Richmond Friends Meeting
May 13, 2018 » Richmond, IN

184 Gracious Calling, Ordered Lives: The Faith and Practice of Friends in the Political Maelstrom
North Carolina Yearly
Meeting (Conservative)
July 13, 2018 » Greensboro, NC

204 Quaker Fundraising in Uncertain Times
Quaker Fundraisers Conference
September 30, 2018 » Philadelphia, PA

214 Tumult, Turmoil, and Truth: Vital Quaker Witness Today
Stephen G. Carey Memorial Lecture at Pendle Hill
April 1, 2019 » Media, PA

230 Naming the Truths: Genocide of Indigenous People
November 19, 2019

234 Fierce Love Now and Forever
October 20, 2020

238 A New Season of Hope and Opportunity
December 22, 2020

244 Impeach Trump
January 12, 2021

Table of Contents *(continued)*

248 Insurrection
February 12, 2021

**251 Stop the Violence
Against Asian
Americans**
March 19, 2021

**254 How Can Quakers
Dismantle the Racism–
Militarism Paradigm?**
August 7, 2021

**258 Our Commitment
to Diversity, Equity,
and Inclusion**
August 10, 2021

**262 As Billionaires Grow
Richer, Children
Sleep Hungry**
Religion News Service
September 27, 2021

**266 UN Climate Conference
Underscores Need for
Bold Action in Congress**
October 7, 2021

**270 What 20 Years
(and Counting)
of the War on Terror
Must Teach Us**
Religion News Service
November 1, 2021

274 Hope and Gratitude
FCNL 2021 Annual Meeting
November 20, 2021 »
Washington, DC (Virtual)

292 About Diane Randall

**294 A Minute of Gratitude
for Diane Randall**

*Dedicated to my mother,
Ruth Larsen Randall Benson,
a lifelong educator and public
servant who first taught me
about faith, hope, and love.*

— Diane Randall

Leading with Hope and Building Trust

Foreword by Marge Abbott

When I first met Diane Randall, she was preceded by a wave of enthusiasm about the selection process for a new Friends Committee on National Legislation (FCNL) executive (now general) secretary. Members of the selection committee felt that their work had been rightly led. The unexpected recommendation of a woman little known among FCNL supporters and with little experience with Quaker organizations came to the General Committee with a calm confidence that this was the right person to lead this beloved organization in a time that turned out to be more painfully difficult than any of us imagined.

One of the challenges FCNL places on the staff and volunteers is to shape an Annual Meeting for the time soon after national elections. How do Friends respond in the moment to the exciting prospect of Barack Obama and the unexpected election of Donald Trump? In both instances, I was thankful for the extended time of worship and for a time of singing together rather than listening to others sing.

In such small gestures, Friends bring their faith to the fore, instead of sliding into the anger that permeated so much of Trump's presidency or setting unrealistic expectations from Obama's victory.

Leading with hope. Building trust. This is where, at the 2011 Annual Meeting, Diane started to lay out a vision of FCNL's work, grounded in worship and characterized by such words as bold, strategic, prophetic, powerful, and relentless. Such words have marked her approach for this past decade. These words re-energized and challenged those of us who have devoted long hours attempting to reshape decisions made by the United States Congress. Even more, they have caught the young adults who have shown up in growing numbers for Spring Lobby Weekend each year.

Reaching upcoming generations and giving them the tools and new language to make themselves heard was a central feature of the very successful capital campaign, which raised $17.5 million with a priority of supporting young adults. Diane, in her little red car, was a symbol of this successful effort to build an endowment and create new programs to link together the spiritual strength and practical methods to build FCNL's base across the nation and reach out beyond the confines of our meetings.

Diane has helped us to become more visible in a turbulent world, a world often toxic but yearning for humility and hope. She asks us if we have a faith that is alive today, addressing the problems of this age. Quakers have long shied away from talking about power. Diane asks us to claim the power that comes of standing in the Light of God.

We have all benefited from Diane's willingness to do the *soul work* that is an essential part of facing the sometimes-painful truths that needed to be addressed as Friends examine their response to the hostile political climate of recent years.

She made space for FCNL to look inward on the changes needed in responding to Black Lives Matter, compounded by the complexities of adjusting to the realities of a pandemic.

Her willingness to make sure that her faith is visible—not just among Quakers, but in places like the Congressional Prayer Breakfast—is a gift to all of us. It is also a reminder that others find ways to make visible how their faith shapes their response to racism and violence.

The contents of this collection, *Leading with Faith, Hope, and Love*, comprise an impressive compendium of important issues where Friends have a distinctive message to share.

I, for one, am most thankful for Diane's leadership and for her friendship that have made a real difference in the world as well as in individual lives like mine. The works included in this volume do much to tell the story that Friends must tell and enlighten us with her sense of passionate humility.

Marge Abbott
Author and former clerk, FCNL General Committee

Marge Abbott photo by Kate Holt/FCNL

Growth Anchored in Faith

Essay by Adlai Amor

"This organization ... is a community, and there are so many people who feel connected and committed to this community— not because of me, but because of what we stand for and what we do. It's true of the people who come to work here and of the people who advocate with us. That's a remarkable foundation for the next general secretary. I feel very good about being part of the FCNL community and having had the opportunity to lead it."

— *Diane Randall, FCNL general secretary, 2011–2021*

While walking home from the office one day, shortly after she began working at FCNL, Diane was stopped in her tracks by a clear internal message echoing Hebrew 11:1, "Now faith is the substance of things hoped for, the evidence of things not seen." She remembers the event distinctly and the spot in front of the U.S. Capitol where she recognized the voice of Spirit, encouraging her in the work of FCNL.

She had no idea how much her faith in a loving, compassionate God would be her strong anchor in the ten years she served as FCNL general secretary. It was an unprecedented decade marked by political, partisan turmoil in Congress, unending war, surging migration worldwide, great social movements, chaotic elections, gaping wealth inequality, an insurrection on Capitol Hill, a renewed recognition of white supremacy and structural racism, an ongoing pandemic, and the calamitous effects of climate change.

Throughout all the turmoil, Diane's faith and hope, joined with the persistent and prophetic work of generations of the FCNL community, provided solid ground for the organization to flourish. Under her leadership, Washington's oldest registered religious lobby experienced a period of immense growth. This was not only because the needs were many, but also that a growing band of ordinary, yet faithful, prophets proved that they could do extraordinary things.

Diane came to FCNL in March 2011 from Partnership for Strong Communities, a nonprofit organization advocating for solutions to homelessness, affordable housing, and community development in Connecticut. A convinced Quaker, she had never considered working for a Quaker organization, but the opportunity to make the spiritual-political connection professionally intrigued her. Upon accepting the position, Diane, her husband, and children relocated to Washington, D.C., so she could embark on her new role as FCNL's fourth—and first woman—general secretary in its then-68-year history.

Her tenure began shortly before the 10-year anniversaries of the 9/11 bombings and subsequent invasions of Iraq and Afghanistan. For nearly a decade prior, FCNL had maintained a steady drumbeat of advocacy around the theme, "War Is Not the Answer." By the time she arrived,

Diane observed that message starting to take hold. There was a noticeable shift in language and tone in the media and on Capitol Hill denoting growing disapproval of the ubiquitous "War on Terror."

During that same time, the United States began to evolve its approach to military engagement around the globe— from drones and special forces to funding weapons sales that fueled humanitarian crises. With an understanding of what resonated on Capitol Hill (and what did not), in light of this change, FCNL had already begun adjusting its strategy as well. It worked to lobby Congress to take back from the president its constitutional authority to declare war and to shift the foreign policy focus in Congress from fearful response to peaceful prevention of violent conflict.

A Long-Game Policy

This pivot would prove beneficial in achieving the *long-game* policy wins FCNL has become known for. After lobbying for state legislative changes, Diane observed, "[C]oming to work in Washington with Congress, things are so slow. It takes a long time to move legislation, but once it does, it has such monumental change—for people throughout the U.S. and often throughout the world."

One of these changes occurred in July 2015 with the signing of the landmark Joint Comprehensive Plan of Action (JCPOA), otherwise known as the Iran nuclear agreement. FCNL's networks and staff lobbyists had been pushing President Barack Obama and Congress to use diplomacy to put the brakes on Iran's nuclear program. FCNL had long worked to prevent war with Iran. Diane's predecessor,

Joe Volk, traveled to Iran in 2007 with a faith delegation that met with then-President Mahmoud Ahmadinejad. Following the 2018 withdrawal by President Trump from the JCPOA, FCNL continued its advocacy to prevent war. Diane and other faith leaders met with Javad Zarif, then Iran's foreign minister, during the United Nations summit in New York City following the 2018 UN General Assembly.

In 2019, after 15 years of faithful advocacy by FCNL and our coalition partners, the 115th Congress passed the Elie Wiesel Genocide and Atrocities Prevention Act (P.L. 115-441), which President Donald Trump subsequently signed into law. Named for a Holocaust survivor, it ensures coordination among U.S. government departments to prevent global atrocities from occurring. It also mandates training for American diplomats to identify early warning signs of genocide.

In the decade after 9/11 and the global war on terror, FCNL's focus on preventing and ending war meant a smaller focus on domestic policy. With her state-level policy experience, Diane encouraged the growth of FCNL's domestic portfolio by building greater organizational capacity to hire more lobbyists. This included seizing the opportunity to lobby for criminal justice reform to reduce long federal prison sentences for nonviolent crimes and to provide better rehabilitation programs for those in prison.

Victory came when the FIRST STEP Act (P.L. 115- 391) was signed into law in December 2018. Although the bill is far from perfect, the FIRST STEP Act was a critical bill in efforts to reform the U.S. criminal justice system.

When Diane arrived at FCNL, operations were well-established in a lovely LEED certified building on Capitol Hill. Six years earlier, FCNL completed restoration of the once-decrepit office building, portions of which date back to the Civil War. Raising substantial funds for the first green building on Capitol Hill was an act of faith, vision, and commitment.

That same faith, vision, and commitment led FCNL's General Committee to establish a Futures Working Group to begin imagining how the organization would thrive into the future by also building out its young adult program. However, the Great Recession paused all new initiatives in 2008–10.

Upon Diane's 2011 arrival, FCNL was ready to pick that work back up. At the same time, there were additional opportunities for growth, including purchasing and renovating the building adjacent to the office (205 C Street). To achieve these goals, FCNL launched a new capital campaign: "The World We Seek: Now Is the Time."

The campaign, which sent Diane around the country to meet donors and speak at Quaker meetings (35 presentations in 17 months!), was successful. It raised $17.5 million for FCNL's programs, including an expanded and revitalized young adult program, a revitalized Friend in Washington program, creation of the Quaker Welcome Center, and an increase in FCNL's endowment.

According to Diane, the campaign's success "was really a validation from donors ... of FCNL's work, fostering a sense of gratitude and sparking our imaginations to live into that trust. People were very keen about the young adult work we were doing."

Investing in Young Adults

With Diane's leadership, FCNL augmented its young adult programs which, she said, "were already well-established and successful." Launched as an internship program during the time that Ed Snyder served as FCNL's second executive secretary, the FCNL Program Assistants program (formerly called the Young Fellows) has become an ingrained part of FCNL life.

Every year, 7-10 recent graduates apply to work with the organization's legislative, strategic advocacy, or Quaker outreach teams. FCNL also began widely promoting Spring Lobby Weekend, tripling its annual attendance since 2011. And in 2015, FCNL further expanded its programming to establish an eight-week, paid summer internship for college students.

FCNL also created the Advocacy Corps in 2015, which Diane credits younger staff for conceptualizing and initiating. This 10-month program pays young adults between 19 and 30 years old to organize in their local communities on one of FCNL's legislative priorities. After taking part in a week-long immersive training in community organizing, media outreach, and lobbying, organizers commit 25 hours monthly to educating and mobilizing their communities to lobby members of Congress for big, long-term change.

Through the Advocacy Corps Program, FCNL is now present in communities where it had not previously been and reaches a more diverse group—or, as Diane says, "more than only Quakers and reaching beyond private liberal arts colleges." She adds, "The program has enriched FCNL with new people and in places we had not previously reached." Advocacy Corps alumni have gone on to secure congressional internships and work for other nonprofit organizations as they hone their leadership and civic participation skills.

"We learn from young adults," Diane says. "The young adult movements that are happening now have so much to teach us. What FCNL can do is provide formal training on effective advocacy, legislation, and connection to Hill offices. I'm really excited about FCNL's future to watch how these programs will strengthen civic engagement and participation in ways our country sorely needs."

As FCNL finished its successful capital campaign, it convened a Forward Planning Working Group in 2016 to seize the opportunities of increased organizational capacity and map five-year strategic goals. Diane worked with both staff and governance, who approved a Forward Plan in 2017. The plan sets five goals for FCNL to grow its presence and power as a Quaker lobby and to take bold steps to transform national policy and decision-making: changing policy; strengthening our strategic advocacy network; expanding media, marketing, and communications; growing our Quaker presence; and ensuring organizational sustainability.

Backed by the commitment of FCNL supporters, governance, and staff, the ambitious Forward Plan allowed FCNL to build greater capacity through investments in staff for our lobbying on the Hill, our engagement of advocates across the country, Quaker outreach, and media and marketing. It also established a stronger administrative foundation for FCNL, the FCNL Education Fund, and the newly acquired Friends Place on Capitol Hill (formerly William Penn House).

Pivoting During a Pandemic

FCNL found other growth opportunities amid the uncertainty of the Covid-19 pandemic. It was a crash course on how to quickly pivot from an office-based organization to one that functions well virtually. Investments in new technologies enabled FCNL to be fully connected with Capitol Hill and people across the country, successfully holding virtual meetings and conferences for up to 600 people at a time.

Both staff and committee members have felt the loss of in-person connection during the pandemic. As Diane says, "We are in a relationship business—with one another and in how we teach people to advocate—it's all about building relationships." Nonetheless, the inability to travel and required social distancing created an efficiency in our advocacy and allowed FCNL to teach hundreds more how to effectively lobby virtually.

Through strategic investments and diligent outreach, FCNL has more than doubled its active online network of advocates. Coupled with digital marketing techniques, the organization is attracting more people—most of whom do not know Quakers—to join its ranks as advocates, donors, or both.

Through this period of growth, Diane believes what has helped to ground the staff—which has increased to over 50 people as of late 2021—has been its enduring sense of community and commitment to advocating for the world we seek. As the world locked down and the United States faced some of its most traumatic challenges in recent history, Diane helped the FCNL community focus on addressing diversity, equity, and inclusion, reflecting specifically on how to unite people whose backgrounds and experiences differ.

Seeking a society with equity and justice for all is built into FCNL's vision, and advocating for policies to end systemic racism have long been part FCNL's legislative priorities. Yet FCNL, like the Religious Society of Friends and society at large, is called to root out the practices that perpetuate white supremacy culture. Diane says, "The focus on becoming a more diverse, equitable, and inclusive organization is essential for FCNL—in our interactions with one another, and through every aspect of how we live into the world."

This is a time marred by significant income and racial disparities, dangerous and divisive language among those in the highest offices of the country, violence, humanitarian crises domestically and abroad, and persistent threats to our democracy at large. We also face an immediate global imperative of addressing the climate crisis. As one senior member of Congress recently told FCNL Advocacy Teams: "We need the Friends."

Diane believes that "FCNL's grounding in Quaker faith and practice—'to see what love can do'—will always distinguish FCNL; this intentionality to practice faith, hope, and love during political turmoil gives deep meaning to our advocacy."

Looking forward, Diane hopes FCNL can continue to equip people around the country to "leaven, ... to use a Biblical term, their practices of civic engagement within their own communities to help government ... function by the people and for the people."

"Leavening" Civic Engagement

One approach to this "leavening" is the FCNL Education Fund's undertaking with a neighborhood landmark— Friends Place on Capitol Hill. This learning center and guesthouse, originally called William Penn House, has advanced peace, justice, and environmental stewardship for more than half a century.

It was initiated during Ed Snyder's service as executive secretary, and in 2019, the FCNL Education Fund assumed governance of the building. By 2020, it began investing $2 million in the quest to reimagine and remodel the historic Quaker space to welcome young adults and activists to Capitol Hill for civic engagement programs.

"We have an opportunity to reach out to college-aged, high school, and middle school students, to bring them and other groups to stay at Friends Place and participate in civic engagement programs, to advocate with FCNL for peace, justice, and a sustainable environment," Diane says.

Over the last decade, Diane says she has learned that "FCNL's strength is sometimes in the margins. It's not always in the spotlight." Though there is much to be done to address the exorbitant amounts of Pentagon spending, weapons sales, climate change, and other issues on which FCNL advocates, the fact that conversations *are* taking place, that the voices of FCNL's network from every state are being heard by members of Congress—during a particularly polarizing time in U.S. history—is what perpetuates a sense of hope. "Our relationship-building with congressional offices and with our coalition partners in Washington, D.C., is so important to our persistent faithfulness," she says.

This approach is partly what led the Center for American Progress to name Diane one of the "15 Faith Leaders to Watch in 2020," a recognition she readily deflects to the whole of FCNL.

Recalling one of her first FCNL executive committee meetings, she tells the story of a member who came to her and said, "Diane, we're so happy you're here. It's going to be great having you here; you are going to be a great leader for FCNL … but it's not all about you. FCNL's power comes from all the people who work here, and who have worked here, the people across the country who advocate with FCNL and the General Committee, Friends who help discern our policies and priorities. The strength of the organization is the community."

"And this has been true," she says. "Our strength is our community choosing hope, acting for justice, believing in peace, striving together for the world we seek."

Adlai Amor is FCNL's associate general secretary for communications. This essay was written with the assistance of Kristen Archer.

Powerful Beyond Measure:
Trusting the Call to Leadership, Exercising Our Citizenship

Philadelphia Yearly Meeting » July 28, 2011 » Philadelphia, PA

*T*his is such a rich subject—the idea of being powerful beyond measure and trusting our call to leadership. I titled these remarks, "Powerful Beyond Measure: Trusting the Call to Leadership/ Exercising Our Citizenship," but the alternate name I came up with was "Everything I Needed to Know About Leadership, I Learned from Quakers."

Assuming there may be people in this Meeting who might find dissonance between Quakerism and leadership, I would like you to consider three key practices of both our faith and of leadership: listening, trusting, and acting. These three practices or qualities are so common for most Quakers they are almost second nature.

We don't think of these as leadership qualities, just as we probably don't think of practicing citizenship as a form of leadership. However, exercising our citizenship is a way of exercising leadership. And these disciplines—listening, trusting, and acting—which aren't unique to Quakers but are pervasive throughout the Quaker experience, are disciplines that we must intentionally practice daily. The result of good exercise is that we get stronger when we practice. We become more powerful.

I am a convinced Quaker—convinced that the Spirit of the Divine is present in my life, that the powerful love of God is meant for me and for every person, and that the discipline and practice of the Religious Society of Friends offers me a way to be in the world.

I had an early sense of justice, not unnatural for a child. Children who are loved usually have a strong instinct for fairness. In my childhood, the images I watched on the evening news—the war in Vietnam and the struggle for racial equality during the civil rights era—moved me. The idea that our country's soldiers were killing people and being killed in a war halfway across the world for an unclear cause just wasn't rational to me and still isn't.

People being denied equal rights based on skin color just didn't correspond with what I was learning in my Lutheran Sunday School. It was clear to me that the teachings of Jesus had an answer for these injustices and that the answer was to love our neighbors, regardless of race, nationality, religion, or creed.

To be fair, the real title of these remarks should be "Everything I Needed to Know About Leadership,

I Learned from Quakers and My Mom" because she taught me the truths that are effective in leading and in lobbying. She regularly imparted knowledge like "you can win more flies with honey than with vinegar" and "treat others like you would like to be treated."

We were not a politically active family. My parents voted—one a Republican and the other a Democrat—and I sometimes heard them talk about current affairs, but it wasn't until I became an adult and a mother myself that I became active politically. I joined the Nuclear Freeze movement. Hanging around peace activists is a good way to become an engaged citizen.

From those peace activists, I learned that being a good citizen was more than simply voting (of course, all Quakers know that); it included being informed, being public about our beliefs, and persuading others.

But it wasn't until I became a Friend that I learned to listen deeply, to listen to silence, to listen to the context of the speaker; and I began to understand this type of listening as an act of love. As Friends, our practice of listening—to one another, to the Still Small Voice, to the silence—is honed through our discipline. The discipline of deep listening is how we discern, how we hear beyond the words, and how we know God's presence. This is a power beyond measure.

In fact, this quality of listening that we have is what makes the Friends Committee on National Legislation a powerful force for advocacy. In my first week at FCNL in March, I participated in a lobby visit in Sen. Harry Reid's (NV) office with a group of eight advocates and two of his key staff.

The advocates were frustrated with what they perceived as lack of commitment by Senate Democrats to protect vital human services in the Continuing Resolution of the budget, and they wanted Sen. Reid to move his caucus to a stronger position.

Voices grew tighter and the tension in the room became thicker. Then Ruth Flower, FCNL's legislative director, spoke up in her clear, knowledgeable, direct way that not only diffused the tension in the room but also got the issue of cuts to the military budget on the table as part of the solution.

On behalf of FCNL, Ruth outlined six steps Rep. John Boehner (OH-08) and Sen. Reid could take to move us forward in the deficit reduction discussion and through the debt ceiling debate:

1. Reduce discretionary spending with at least half coming from military spending, which has doubled in the last decade. The bipartisan Sustainable Defense Task Force has identified nearly a trillion dollars in military spending reductions that could be adopted over the next ten years without affecting the security of the U.S.

2. Reduce spending through the tax code by closing tax loopholes, especially those that do not promote good public policy as a fair way to raise revenues.

3. End the wars. Both major parties now seem to agree that ending the wars in Afghanistan and Iraq will save about $1 trillion over the next decade.

4. Get a handle on healthcare spending. The Affordable Care Act is projected to decrease the deficit $210 billion over the next decade. Improvements to the system, such as removing for-profit insurance companies from the center of healthcare finance equation, would save even more. Shortsighted changes, such as getting rid of the "CLASS Act"—a provision of the Affordable Care Act that subsidizes and promotes the purchase of home healthcare insurance—will just place more pressure on Medicaid and Medicare programs in the future.

5. Invest in direct job creation. Congress's recent attention to job creation has been primarily on easing the tax burden of employers. More than anything else, small business advocates emphasize that they need customers who can buy their products and services. Unemployed people need jobs before they can be customers.

6. Protect the most vulnerable. The wealthiest one percent of all households lost about 20% of their income in 2008 but the record gap between high and low incomes grew and is still dramatic. Among middle-income households, many lost everything—jobs, homes, savings, healthcare. And among the poorest, many became—and remain—destitute. Thirty-five percent of African American households and 31% of Hispanic households had zero or negative income in 2009. Cutting the services and benefits for the poorest families and individuals is fundamentally unfair and shortsighted.

It is not surprising that another hallmark of vitality among Friends is the trust level within our monthly meetings and yearly meetings. This trust doesn't come easily; we are all human and subject to the foibles of humanity and we sometimes offend each other. But the very nature of our corporate worship is based on trust, trust that in our worship we are led. This is power beyond measure. I find that one of the most hopeful activities I can do is to sit with others, intent on being still enough to listen and to be guided within the Trust of the community.

One of the people I have had occasion to meet since joining FCNL is Robert Levering, a Friend, who conducts Forbes Magazine's "100 Best Companies to Work For." Major national companies vie to be listed, and Levering, along with Amy Lyman, have created the Great Place to Work Institute. Robert has written books and is invited to speak to business audiences around the world. Perhaps it won't surprise you that the common factor that makes companies great places to work is trust. "Trust-based relationships are at the heart of every great workplace," according to the Institute. Count Levering among the list of Quakers who could bring wisdom to Washington.

Lack of trust is one of the problems driving current political debates. There is a lack of trust among political parties, between the House and the Senate, between the White House and Congress, between the tea party and all of government, and the divisions multiply. The media love to amplify this lack of trust because it sells, and it gives bombastic broadcasters and bloggers more to shout about.

Yet, FCNL successfully builds trust. Moreover, we have a legacy of integrity that comes from generations of dedicated Friends governing the organization, from activists who are engaged with FCNL, from our quality staff, from my predecessors—Joe Volk, Ed Snyder, and E. Raymond Wilson—and because we are Quakers.

Here are some examples of what's working right now in Washington that FCNL has helped move forward:

» New resources for nuclear non-proliferation: last week $35 million was added to an account in the Energy/Water appropriations subcommittee through a bipartisan amendment.

» Unlikely suspects calling for cuts to the military budget, including Sen. Coburn of Oklahoma.

» The voices of the faith community being heard in a new way on environmental advocacy—opening doors to more conservative members who won't talk to the "Big Green" lobbyists.

» Growing bipartisan support to end the war in Afghanistan: last month's vote on the McGovern-Jones bill drew significantly more votes than it had in the past two years.

» Approval of funding for the Afghanistan-Pakistan study group in the 2012 Defense Authorization Act.

Behind the scenes, FCNL is shepherding the creation of a genocide-prevention bill among a vital network of protection and prevention organizations, as well as staff of Republican and Democratic senators who have agreed to co-sponsor the legislation. Mary Stata, program assistant in the Peaceful Prevention of Deadly Conflict program, is our lead staff on the bill, which we expect to see introduced before the end of the year. These very important steps are only part of what FCNL is working on right now.

FCNL's call to act comes from the inspiration of Friends across the United States who give input to the policies and priorities proposed by Quaker meetings and churches. We bring a voice of hope and possibility for a world that is better than the one we inhabit:

» We are lifting the inspiring vision of a world without war and the threat of war, a society with equity and justice for all, a community where every person's potential may be fulfilled, and an earth restored.

» We are imagining and working pragmatically for what seems politically impossible: a Congress and foreign policy not wed to militarism; peaceful prevention of deadly conflict; an end to nuclear weapons; greenhouse gas reduction; energy policy built on sustainable, renewable sources; an equitable and fair federal budget; and human rights protection for all.

» We are engaging Friends and others who agree with us in a network of 50,000 activists, and we are determined to grow that network.

» We are dedicated to grounding young adults in effective leadership, citizenship, and Quaker lobbying.

FCNL is the most comprehensive faith-based peace and justice lobby in Washington, D.C. We have many colleagues with whom we work closely—other faith-based, national security, human rights, peace, and environmental lobbies—but I'm not aware of many that tie these issues all together.

Looking ahead, I believe it is important for us to weave our witness more effectively in a way that makes the linkages among our programs stronger. Our world is hungry for the values we hold, for having solutions to move forward.

At the same time, it is incumbent on FCNL to continue our historic commitment to engaging young adults through our yearlong internship program and augment this program for the future. Our interns, whom we prefer to call *program assistants* to reflect their level of work more accurately at FCNL, go on to become staffers to members of Congress, policy staff at FCNL and other advocacy organizations, attorneys, business leaders, activists, parents, and members of monthly meetings.

We are considering additional ways to engage young adults, including our 2012 Young Adult Lobby Weekend in March. Based on our 2011 Young Adult Lobby Weekend that included over 100 college-age students who became informed on the war in Afghanistan and how to lobby, and then lobbied, we believe this is a critical constituency and an important role FCNL plays within the Religious Society of Friends and beyond.

Before I conclude, I want to share the advice and encouragement I received during my trip to the Middle East two months ago. I traveled with Jonathan Evans, who has been our foreign policy legislative representative this past year. You may know that our foreign policy program covers the world, with a particular attention to Israel/Palestine.

The 10 days we spent in Jordan, Iraq, and the occupied territories gave me a beginner's understanding of life in those places and a grounding for FCNL's work I would have never had without being there.

We had the opportunity to visit Jim and Debbie Fine, members of this yearly meeting, who are now working in Iraq for the Mennonite Central Committee, along with Ann Ward, another Friend from this yearly meeting. They are based in Ankawa, Iraq, just outside of Erbil. Jim is the former foreign policy legislative secretary at FCNL, who knows the Middle East from decades of experience and speaks Arabic.

The visits Jim and Debbie arranged for us in Erbil and other parts of Kurdish Iraq gave us glimpses of the fragile condition for democracy, freedom, and opportunity that has captured our attention throughout the Middle East and North Africa over the past six months. Their work in peacemaking across fractious ethnic and religious divides inspired us, along with the painstaking work that local leaders are doing to build nongovernmental organizations that promote effective civilian infrastructure.

Our time in Palestine—the West Bank and Gaza—was guided by Jonathan, who not only lived there with his family for several years, but has also been leading Westtown school trips. We spent time with Jean Zaru, clerk of Ramallah Friends Meeting; Kathy Bergen of the Friends International Center; and several others active in Ramallah Friends School—the Play Center; the American Friends Service Committee; the Boycott, Divestment, and Sanctions (BDS) movement; and more. We visited Bethlehem and Hebron and saw the refugee camps, and we saw the separation wall—the 25-foot concrete barrier imposed throughout neighborhoods in the West Bank.

Diane and a War Is Not the Answer sign painted on the separation wall next to the Wi'am office in Bethlehem. Our understanding is that this sign was painted by the Young Adult group that traveled to Israel/Palestine in the summer of 2006 under the auspices of Philadelphia Yearly Meeting's Middle East Working Group.

The Ramallah Meeting House/Friends International Center in Ramallah (FICR). From left to right: Muna Khleifi (supervisor, Quaker Play Center in Amari Refugee Camp), Kathy Bergen (FICR program coordinator), Diane Randall, Jonathan Evans, Joyce Ajlouny (director of Ramallah Friends School), and Thuqan Qishawi (West Bank director, AFSC).

We went through the extreme checkpoint at Eretz to cross into Gaza—a dusty, impoverished strip of land packed with 1.4 million Palestinians that is as different from Tel Aviv, just 40 kilometers away, as night and day.

Palestinians and Israelis talked to us about human rights, human dignity, and a "just peace." When we told them that our job at FCNL is to talk to the U.S. Congress and asked what we should talk about, Nazim, a Palestinian in Gaza, replied, "Tell them we're human; tell them we're human beings."

Our visit came just days after Israeli Prime Minister Benjamin Netanyahu addressed Congress and received 22 standing ovations. The Palestinians were in disbelief over the seeming adoration that Congress has for a governmental leader imposing a singular agenda that thwarts the opportunities for a two-state solution for Israel and Palestine. Sam Bahour, a Palestinian businessman, said this to us when we asked his advice about our work with Congress: "You have your work cut out for you. There is plenty for you to do in talking with Congress."

I echo the words of my Palestinian friend and encourage you to exercise your citizenship and trust the call to leadership of being an engaged citizen. Don't make the mistake of only talking to each other about politics, about the frustrations you may have, or about your differences with members of Congress and think you've communicated with them. Your elected officials need to hear from you; they need to hear from Friends—even if they think they don't, or even if they dismiss you. You are a constituent; they work for you.

Trust the call to leadership. Exercise your citizenship. Be powerful beyond measure.

Inspired Faith:
Action in a Time of Conflict

FCNL 2011 Annual Meeting » November 8, 2011 » Washington, DC

Before I begin, I want to give a special welcome to my predecessors, Ed Snyder and Joe Volk, whose leadership and stewardship here at FCNL—along with the significant investment of devotion and imagination that so many of you have given to FCNL—have helped shape a remarkable organization.

A year ago, when you approved my appointment as the new executive secretary, I was a bit anxious to come before this General Committee to make remarks. As clearly as I felt led by God, embraced by the search committee, and warmly welcomed by all of you, I didn't quite know what I was getting myself into. Now, after living in Washington for eight months and coming to know FCNL, I can tell you that I'm still a bit anxious—not about FCNL nor about coming into the role of executive secretary; not about speaking to you tonight nor the annual meeting we began today. My anxiety, like much of the rest of the country's, is about Washington.

It's not news to you that the partisan divide is deep, entrenched, and ideological. After the New York Times revealed a couple of weeks ago that the approval rating of Congress was at 8%, one member of Congress asked who were the 8% that thought Congress was doing well. Even the members acknowledge deficiency! But it's not even the partisan conflict that makes me anxious.

What fuels my anxiety is also what makes me realize the monumental call for FCNL; the acquiescence and often bipartisan agreement on a militarized federal budget, a militarized foreign policy, a militarized economic policy, and a militarized energy policy gravely trouble me. It is not just an acceptance among members of Congress, but a structural way of operating; and it's a situation that we the people have allowed. This acceptance of virtually unchecked military growth with profits for contractors, this faith that the military has all the solutions to make our country great, is a broken system.

We have a Congress that, for the last decade through both Republican and Democratic leadership, has increased military spending to such a level that every plan for "cutting" the military budget merely slows its growth.

We have a Congress that has given a blank check to the military to promote generals, launch new military strategies, and secure new weapons, yet is willing to waste $35 billion every year on fraud and mismanagement in the Pentagon.

We have a Congress that is willing to cut healthcare and human services for children and families, yet fails to realize that veterans who have sacrificed their lives are facing rising levels of mental illness, homelessness, and suicide.

We have a Congress that is willing to send American troops to foreign countries to fight, but is simultaneously unwilling to invest in the long view of a changing globe by establishing an energy policy based on renewable sources, an environmental policy that recognizes climate change, and a foreign policy that prevents wars.

I know it's not very Quakerly of me, but I find this outrageous. Fortunately, my better angels prevail most of the time, and I'm able to control the outrage. Even better for me, I have the right job—one that allows me and all of us who are part of FCNL to ground our work in the power that takes away the occasion for all wars. That power, that Light, which brings us hope and daily renewal, is the inspired faith that drives us to seek a world free of war and the threat of war, a society with equity and justice for all, a community where every person's potential may be fulfilled, and an earth restored.

What does it mean to work from inspired faith in a time of conflict? It means recognizing that our work is walking into the conflict and staying clear about our call. It means that to realize the world we seek, we must be bold, strategic, and relentless.

This is no small task we have in front of us, and while we often focus on what is current and the immediate legislation pending, we must also take a long view and consider how we will sustain our witness—our Quaker lobby in the public interest. We need to fortify ourselves.

The Bible reference that came to mind is the "full armor of God," Paul's letter to the Ephesians urging them to become strong against the spiritual forces of evil by putting on "the breastplate of righteousness, the belt of truth, the gospel of peace, the shield of faith, and the sword of the spirit." Although this language and the warrior imagery is jarring for us at FCNL, the notion of girding ourselves is very valid.

Here is how I conceive of FCNL's work to equip ourselves for this inspired faith; how we are bold, strategic, and relentless:

» Our policies and priorities are grounded in the Religious Society of Friends, discerned through listening worship.

» Our governing body is led, centered, and devoted.

» Our staff is wise, persistent, and persuasive.

» We have a young adult presence that is passionate, energetic, and smart.

» We are supported by donors and grassroots activists who are dedicated and caring.

With this kind of equipment, we can move mountains!

Beyond this fall, beyond the election year, we must look at FCNL within the arc of history and the future We must evaluate how FCNL is squarely in the procession of Friends who have been bold, strategic, and relentless in their advocacy for peace and justice.

Most of you in this room tonight have a broad understanding of FCNL's historic work because many of you have lived it. You have seen the importance of our role in successful initiatives that have advanced policies and programs for peace. There are three initiatives that have been part of our history and that I hope will grow in the coming years:

» Our Young Adult program

» Our Friend in Washington program

» Growing Our Network: presence among Friends and friends

The internship program, which has operated for over 35 years, has provided FCNL with young, energetic workers who have assisted our programs on foreign policy, Native American affairs, immigration, the federal budget, the environment, peaceful prevention of deadly conflict, nuclear disarmament, and communications and campaigns. I have had the opportunity to work with two classes of program assistants and have seen firsthand the vitality they bring to FCNL and the knowledge and skills they carry with them when they leave.

Moreover, we have realized the benefit of many former program assistants who now serve on FCNL's staff and on our General Committee. Some have gone on to lead policy operations for members of Congress, within the administration, or with other nonprofit organizations. All have been affected in positive ways; many have been transformed by their experience.

FCNL has so much to gain by fortifying this program—by guaranteeing that we have a solid cadre of interns each year and assuring that the young adults who give a year's time have the opportunities and experiences that make them bold, strategic, and relentless in their quest for peace and justice in whatever profession they choose. These program assistants, who are so much more than interns, are the FCNL alumni; they are our field team; they are inspirational. Staying engaged with our former program associates creates a network for them and us.

Another opportunity to expand our work with young adults is through our Spring Lobby Weekend, which has grown each of the past seven years. It provides those who come from Quaker schools like Haverford, Wilmington, and Earlham, as well as those who have a passion for peace and justice and want a taste of effective advocacy, an opportunity to be in Washington, learn an issue, learn how to lobby, and practice lobbying.

What if 1,000 young adults gathered under FCNL's training each spring to lobby against the war in Afghanistan, for immigration reform, or for real climate change legislation? Moreover, what if these 19- and 20-year-olds who participate determine that, whatever they do in life, they would work to build relationships with elected officials to relentlessly press for positive policy changes? What if some of them decide that the most strategic way to effect change is to run for public office?

Imagine the possibilities for engaging youth and young adults in the ways FCNL speaks to Quaker concerns on Capitol Hill. We must consider how to recruit interns so that we have a more diverse constituency in the young adult program. Perhaps there are ways to work with high-

Leading with Hope, Faith, and Love: The Diane E. Randall Collection

school-age students who want to learn lobbying with other Quaker organizations like William Penn House or Yearly Meeting Young Friends groups.

A couple of weeks ago, I visited George Fox University in Portland, Oregon, to speak to students and the public about FCNL. As I was speaking enthusiastically about the young adults working at FCNL, a young man in the audience identified himself as a 13-year-old, home-schooled student who had been researching the death penalty and humanitarian issues.

"What are the opportunities for someone my age to participate with FCNL's lobbying?", he asked. "Come to the Spring Lobby Weekend!" was my response. Why not find ways to engage those who are hungry to use their voices to guide the decisions that will affect their future? Our boldness is not only in our prophetic witness, but also in creatively imagining the possibilities for our work ahead.

While my admiration for the energy and engagement of the young adults who work with FCNL as staff and in our governance is well-known, I have many hopes about the wisdom of experience in our midst.

Many of you on the General Committee are familiar with the Friend in Washington program; some of you have been Friends in Washington working for FCNL while others have supported the program. The program's impact is significant and extends over decades. The groundbreaking work of Sam and Miriam Levering over 35 years ago on behalf of FCNL for the Law of the Seas is well-known.

A few months ago, David Culp got a call from Sen. John Kerry's staff looking to build a network of people who would help organize efforts to seek ratification of that treaty.

We have begun thinking about possibilities of how we might once again operate a Friend in Washington program, examining how it has worked in the past and how we could tap our Quaker network for the wisdom and focused dedication that Friends would bring to FCNL priorities through a short-term residency program at FCNL.

Opportunities might include conducting research, mentoring young adults, offering spiritual support, writing policy briefs, or creating educational opportunities for colleagues and Hill staffers. It is exciting to consider the possibilities for strategically using our Quaker network to bring intelligence and influence for a time in Washington. It is also exciting to consider how these Friends in Washington return home to their local communities with inspiration to engage others.

Growing our network among Friends and friends has become increasingly important to getting the attention of members of Congress. FCNL has made important strides in this area. We ask a lot of our network; our Campaigns team and Field Committee can vouch for that.

We ask them to read a lot of email and respond to a lot of action alerts. We ask them to give money. We ask our General Committee to add an extra day onto Annual Meeting to lobby, and we ask people to set up meetings in-district to lobby. We ask people to climb the ladder of engagement—to develop ongoing relationships with their lawmakers' offices on behalf of the key FCNL priorities.

You might even say we are bold, strategic, and relentless in what we ask of our network. But I think we can do more, and given our vision of the world we seek, we must.

What if there were an FCNL person in every congressional district so when we need to lobby Rep. Kay Granger of Texas on the Complex Crises Fund or get to Rep. David Camp of Michigan on renewable energy subsidies, a constituent who knows the member could make the call? Then that constituent could engage others in the district to influence the members. Consistent voices make a difference, and we aim to grow the number of voices.

My hope is to have an FCNL network that includes contacts in each of the 435 congressional districts. I'd like to see grassroots lobbyists in every state who are trained in Quaker lobbying and are willing to encourage others in their communities to join them in being in regular, consistent contact with their members.

These grassroots contacts bolster the work of our Hill team. There is no substitution for effective, ongoing relationships with members of Congress and their staffs. That happens through the repeated contacts and expertise of our lobbyists. The inside knowledge that comes from our presence on Capitol Hill—from participating in coalitions, sharing information and ideas with other lobbyists and staff—is at the heart of FCNL. It is why we need steady support for our organization.

We will continue to invest in a full lobbying team that has the capacity to represent our priorities effectively. This core function of FCNL advances the priorities and policies that come through our meetings and churches and are established through the discernment of this body. Fortifying our lobbying through a robust young adult program, a focused Friend in Washington program, and a dynamic network of engaged Friends will make FCNL even stronger than it is today.

Friends, you are here because of your faithfulness at a time of conflict, conflict that includes Congress and political leaders who have accepted a militarized framework for too many of our public policies; partisan divide over whether the role of government should benefit the common good; continuous growth of economic disparity between the very rich, the shrinking middle class, and the poor; and nonviolent movements for change in North Africa and the Middle East.

Some of our faithfulness in a time of conflict is to welcome the conflict as a means of shifting a paradigm and reframing our worldview. The acceleration of news and information to an instantaneous timeframe means that we are in constant motion. It has also lifted and connected people who might not have considered themselves allies through their recognition of shared values, aspirations, and demands.

We see people rethinking the status quo. In this year alone, we have seen the emergence of dynamic changes in the Arab Spring actions, the Occupy movement, and the opposition to the Tar Sands pipeline that now have the president's attention. These eruptions of democracy in action are encouraging, particularly as we see our fellow travelers exercising tools of nonviolence and decision-making that we value so deeply. This is inspired faith.

Thank you for your faithfulness in this time of conflict. Thank you for your lobbying, for your dedication to FCNL, for making time to be here, for your financial support, for your moral support of staff, and for your prayers.

Before I end, let me be bold and ask for this: I want you to do something that we don't normally associate with Quakerism these days, but some of you already do it.

I want you to proselytize for FCNL. When you go back to Denver, Olympia, Ann Arbor, Wilmington, or wherever your home is, tell your own meetings and churches how you spent the weekend, and tell them why they ought to get involved with FCNL. Tell them how easy it is to act if they sign up for our emails (and tell them they don't have act on everything).

Your help is essential in advancing the world wee seek by explaining who FCNL is and why its work is important to the Religious Society of Friends and to friends who want to create a better world. Your representation in your monthly meetings and churches, in your yearly meetings, to your family and friends speaks volumes.

In addition to relying on so many of you as living FCNL historians, I have been reading E. Raymond Wilson's *Uphill for Peace*. I leave you with the words that open his book:

"Why try to work uphill for peace, justice, and freedom on Capitol Hill at a time when cynicism about the character and operation of government and government officials is widespread, and when disillusionment about the church and organized religion is so common and so vocal? Because religion should be vital and relevant and because the health and the future of democracy rests upon responsible participation by informed and concerned citizens.

"A world without war, without conscription and militarism has still to be achieved. Even in the United States, the price of liberty is still eternal vigilance. The battle for justice is never-ending. A world dominated by military, economic, and political power easily forgets fairness and compassion for the disadvantaged and dispossessed at home and abroad.

"To strive for these and similar goals has been the role of Friends Committee on National Legislation."

There is such ripeness for our work; for our bold, strategic, and relentless exercise of our democracy; for our persistent, persuasive, prophetic, and pragmatic operation on Capitol Hill and throughout the country.

Faith and Public Action

William Penn University » September 18, 2012 » Oskaloosa, IA

I am pleased to be addressing you today in convocation at the launch of your school year and amid national elections.

I live and work in Washington, D.C., and it seems that the path from Washington to Iowa and back is well established. During the election season, which is covered by the media intensely for a year prior to the actual popular vote, Iowa is the epicenter. From the early caucuses in January to remaining in the *swing state* column for candidates, this state sees a lot of campaigning.

I am here today to talk less about politics and more about public policy; to talk about citizenship and the role of faith in public life. As the head of a Quaker lobby organization that works to influence public policy in Washington,

I am an ardent believer that citizen engagement makes the world a better place. I believe citizen engagement is central to what you are learning here at William Penn University. The knowledge you gain through your classes, reading, writing, and production of ideas, may be at the core of your intellectual development—just as living, working, and volunteering with and among others who are different than you and being exposed to ideas that may seem alien to you are at the core of your emotional and social development.

Your college experience—in the classroom, in your residential life, on the athletic fields, and through clubs and activities—builds community; and your friendships and the relationships you develop during your time at William Penn will help shape who you are. Some of these relationships may be lifelong—like meeting the person you will marry; developing best friends; or being inspired by a professor, coach, or administrator. Other relationships will be transient and transactional.

Learning to live, play, and work with others who are different from you can be one of the most significant experiences college offers. Figuring out how to have respectful relationships and civil dialogue with people you disagree with, and may not even like, is a fundamental step to good citizenship.

When I was a child, I thought being a good citizen simply meant voting in every election. While I still believe that is one of the most fundamental rights we exercise as good citizens, through my life, I have seen how much more citizenship means. Travel to any other country, engage with the international students on your campus, and you will

Leading with Hope, Faith, and Love: The Diane E. Randall Collection

find yourself having to think through your own beliefs, hopes, and definition of citizenship.

Let me give you examples of what I see as good citizenship:

» Respecting the property of others.

» Obeying traffic laws.

» Being a good neighbor.

» Making your community a more attractive place to live through quality-of-life solutions like picking up litter or establishing a community garden.

» Volunteering to help others who are vulnerable— children, the elderly, people with disabilities.

» Speaking out for civil and human rights of every person.

» Working for the election of a candidate you believe in.

» Running for public office.

» Advocating with public officials for changes in public policy.

» Listening and engaging in dialogue with your fellow citizens on issues where you disagree.

I am guessing that most of you would agree with every item on this list as good citizenship; indeed, many of you may participate in every one of these activities—perhaps except for running for public office, though I would encourage you to keep that option open because good leaders with integrity and imagination are always needed in public life.

At the Friends Committee on National Legislation (FCNL), our work is about the last two items on that list:

» Listening and engaging in dialogue with our fellow citizens on issues where we disagree.

» Advocating with public officials for changes in public policy.

FCNL advocates in Washington, D.C., with Congress and the administration for priorities established by Friends meetings and churches across the country. What does this mean?

You know from being a student at a Quaker college that certain *testimonies* guide our faith: simplicity, peace, integrity, community, and equality. Every two years, FCNL asks Quaker meetings and churches throughout the United States to engage in dialogue within their communities— to give us guidance as to what our priorities should be in lobbying Congress.

The idea that our faith influences our public actions is central to most religions; in the Christian tradition this is most simply laid out in Jesus' admonition to "love your neighbor as yourself." Quakers have historically carried our concerns to try to influence policies for peace and justice— both at the local, immediate community level and beyond.

Individual Quakers have often been early leaders in the struggle for equality—ending slavery, voting rights for women, abolition of the death penalty—and as a faith community, we have frequently found unity in the work to advance peace and promote justice. During its nearly 70-year history, FCNL's lobby helped establish the Peace Corps and Civil Rights Act in the 1960s and more recently, helped secure Senate ratification of the New START treaty.

By no means have Friends historically had total agreement on the issues that divide our country politically. But Friends across the country do support a wide range of activism and social and financial investment in peace and justice, in good citizenship. At FCNL, we have wide support from Quakers and others who are like-minded on a range of foreign and domestic policy issues.

From lobbying to end the war in Afghanistan and pressing lawmakers to address the devastating effects of climate change, to promoting the peaceful prevention of deadly conflict, FCNL lobbyists work to change U.S. policies. So what does this look like from Washington and from Oskaloosa, and what does it have to do with citizenship and William Penn University?

In Washington, we have about 30 staff working at the FCNL office, which is located on Capitol Hill—just about two blocks from the Capitol and across the street from the Hart Senate Office Building, where Sen. Harkin's and Sen. Grassley's offices are located. Two-thirds of our staff are under 30 years old; seven of them graduated from college in May and just started working at FCNL two weeks ago in an 11-month internship program.

Faith and Public Action

These interns, or program assistants as their business cards read, are assigned to a specific issue or program area— Afghanistan, the federal budget, immigration, Native American concerns, sustainable energy and environment, nuclear disarmament, communications, coordinating office volunteers, outreach to contacts in Quaker meetings and churches, and even the "War Is Not the Answer" sign and bumper sticker distribution.

We have one intern who stayed with us for a second year to continue supporting our efforts to prevent war with Iran and the peaceful prevention of deadly conflict. We have another intern organizing our recruitment for participation in FCNL's Quaker Public Policy Institute, which will take place November 15-16 in Washington, D.C., during the lame-duck session of Congress.

These young adults have parlayed their college experiences into work that will help develop their experience as well as their professional networks in policy, advocacy, and communications. I share this because all of you who are students will be figuring out what your next step is beyond William Penn University; some of you must figure this out soon, while others may have four years to relish your learning before you plan what comes next.

Many of you will go immediately to work and will continue to develop your good citizenship as an employee, neighbor, parent, or member of a church. Some of you may choose to explore the idea of working in Washington for a year with FCNL, going abroad to volunteer for an international service project, working for Teach for America, participating in Quaker Volunteer

Service, or volunteering with AmeriCorps on projects that build better communities. These experiences, which are not financially lucrative, provide you with another kind of capital—social capital in exposing yourself to a world that is different from your own.

Often, it is these direct experiences of seeing the suffering or challenges of our fellow human beings that motivate us to work on public policy.

We begin to ask questions of *why*? Why should I be entitled to a great education when girls in Afghanistan are not allowed to learn to read? Why is this family in Des Moines homeless when my family has a safe, secure home? Why do these villages in Kenya have no running water? Why do people in this country go to bed hungry when we have vast agricultural resources? Why do we fight wars on borrowed money?

In fact, some of the questions of public policy will be very personal: Will I get a job when I graduate from college? Will my dad or mom be able to keep their jobs? How will I ever be able to afford to own a home? What concerns you in public policy will be affected by your own circumstances and experiences, and it may be affected by your faith.

At FCNL, our Quaker faith leads us to apply our testimonies to lobby for a more peaceful and just world. This means reducing reliance on the military for responding to conflict and promoting the tools of development and diplomacy that can prevent deadly conflict. It means lobbying for funding increases for programs in the State Department that promote civilian peacemaking and lobbying for decreases in the

Faith and Public Action

military budget that dwarfs our expenditures on diplomacy. It means lobbying to protect domestic programs that invest in solutions to poverty and protect people who are vulnerable— the elderly, children, people with disabilities, veterans.

It means lobbying for the recognition that confronting climate change has a moral dimension. It is not just for our well-being, but for our children and future generations who will live on a planet with climate disruptions that threaten livelihood and lives and can lead to deadly conflict over disputes for natural resources.

It means talking to all elected officials, including those who might not agree with us. In fact, many of our priorities are difficult political choices. Our work as lobbyists in Washington and our encouragement to Friends and others who are part of FCNL's network throughout the country is to build relationships with elected officials, just as we build relationships in our communities. Building respectful relationships is the foundation of good citizenship.

My faith and practice as a member of the Religious Society of Friends has shaped me and encourages me to take that idea one step further; to not just be respectful but to listen with love, especially to those who believe differently than I do.

One of my favorite Quaker quotes comes from the Journal of John Woolman, a great spiritual leader whose writing describes his travels among Friends in the 1700s. Woolman's Journal reveals a rich inner life that contemplates the problems of his day—particularly slavery and relationships with Indian tribes.

In this passage from 1763, amid the French and Indian War, he writes on his way to visit the Indians of Wyalusing in Pennsylvania:

> *"Love was the first motion, and then a concern arose to spend some time with the Indians, that I might feel and understand their life and the spirit they live in, haply I might receive some instruction from them, or they be in any degree helped forward by my following the leadings for Truth among them."*

When I read, "Love was the first motion," I think of the lives that speak to me—both those who are famous for letting love be the first motion, like John Woolman, Mahatma Gandhi, or Martin Luther King Jr., as well as people I know who demonstrate care and compassion and Jesus' commandment to "love your neighbor as yourself."

There are thousands of actions we can take throughout our lives that make us good citizens and contribute to the common good. Today, the rest of this year, and throughout your career at William Penn, I encourage you to practice good citizenship.

Let your life speak by the actions you take to make your community a better place. Start with your campus; listen to those who are different, those you disagree with, and see if you can find common ground. Learn about Islam and what is causing the turmoil in Arab countries.

Talk to your fellow students from Rwanda and hear what has shaped their lives. Those of you who are from small towns and those of you from cities: share stories about your family life or your neighborhoods with each other.

What are the problems on campus? Advocate for changing these problems with solutions that make life better for everyone.

Along the way, I want to invite you to engage in public policy. Join us at FCNL. You can sign up to receive our action alerts by going to our website, *www.fcnl.org*, or you can become more active and join us in Washington, D.C., to lobby with us at our Quaker Public Policy Institute in November or at our Young Adult Spring Lobby Weekend next March along with students from other college campuses.

Whether or not you get active with FCNL, I hope you will always consider how you might practice good citizenship, how you might keep yourself open to new experiences right now in your life at William Penn and throughout your lives. Cultivate your inner life as John Woolman did and consider how you might let love be the first motion.

Power from Knowing God

Congressional Prayer Breakfast of the Churches for Middle East Peace
May 21, 2013 » Washington, DC

I am honored to be with you this morning. I was pleased that Warren Clark and Doris Warrell contacted me to offer a reflection as we prepare to go to the Hill to engage members of Congress and their staffs on peace and justice in Israel and Palestine. I am a Quaker but was raised as a Lutheran and find great comfort and encouragement in the faith traditions that have nurtured me.

I worship in the unprogrammed tradition of Friends in which we gather for worship to enjoy both silent and vocal ministry. Our intention of listening deeply together for the movement of the Spirit forms us.

I want to talk this morning about power and weave into my message a reflection of what I heard several of yesterday's speakers say about power. Specifically, I want to reflect on the effective use of power—not that which comes from holding elective office, the power that comes from having a lot of money, or the power that comes from celebrity status of those we regularly see in the media.

I want to talk about the effective use of power that comes from knowing God and living life from the inside out.

In the 1640s, during a time of religious foment in England, George Fox, the founder of the Religious Society of Friends, was dissatisfied with the clergy and the churches of his day. He just didn't accept the fact that his spiritual welfare depended on his role with the church.

In some ways, his discontent is not unlike the discontent we see from young people today who don't adhere to institutional structures, but long for peace and justice. Here is what George Fox asked those he was preaching to:

> *"You will say, Christ sayest this and the apostles sayest this; but what cans't thou say? Art thou a child of light and hast thou walked in the Light and what thou speakest, is it inwardly from God?"*

In my interpretation, George Fox was asking how our direct experience with God informs our lives. He was not asking what the church was teaching or which way the political wind was blowing. He was not asking what the experts say or what we have been told; rather, what does our own experience of knowing the Light and the Spirit, and of practicing love move us toward? What evidence does God manifest in our lives?

As Rev. Bob Roberts said yesterday when he spoke about kingdom theology, the words of Jesus are quite clear. I am not a theologian, so I cannot speak to that as a theological system of beliefs other than to say this: when I began working at the Friends Committee on National Legislation and considered our vision of a world without war and the threat of war, a community where every person's potential may be fulfilled, a society with equity and justice for all, and an earth restored, I realized I had a lifetime of work before me—to seek peace, justice, empowerment, and healing. This is the work that the inward movement of the Spirit in our lives directs us to.

I was talking with a friend last week who is a spiritual director and who talked about our ways of knowing. We have head knowledge and heart knowledge, but we also have knowledge in our gut and in our bones. I think of the knowledge in our bones as the deep, generational connections that hunger for justice, know peace is the way, and have a universality of our kindred spirits.

This knowledge is the basis of relationship. Bob Roberts talked about relationships as the foundation of the development assistance and interfaith and foreign policy work he and his church undertake—not political work, but human work that engages people to pursue human security.

Leila Hilal spoke yesterday about the mass movements of young adults longing for fairness and having the democratic means to build civil society from a framework of nonviolence. The power of social networks spawned by communication technology and innovation is rapidly changing our world; information that was once available to only a few is now available to all, and we are seeing new ways to be in the world—ways of nonviolence and democratic rule. This movement of a younger generation creating social networks can build peace and offer a core foundation for protecting human rights. This work builds power.

Last year, I had the opportunity to spend a couple of weeks in Kenya, first at an international gathering of Quakers and then with Friends who are part of Friends Church Peace Teams and African Great Lakes Initiative. These Friends, who were conducting trainings using an Alternatives to Violence program, worked alongside other people of faith and civil society actors for peaceful solutions to deadly conflict, healing, and reconciliation for past violence.

This work has been going on for several years, but accelerated following the 2007-2008 election violence that resulted in the deaths of 1,000 people and the displacement of tens of thousands more. One of the Kenyan women trainers who spoke to our group declared with a confident forthrightness and inward knowing, "I am an agent for peace." This agency for peace inspires us, provides a practical way to implement positive change, and offers a kind of power that can change hearts and minds.

Throughout Israel, Palestine, and the United States, there are agents of peace, building both the small and large steps that create change. Last week, I had the opportunity to meet a Palestinian businessman, an Israeli businesswoman, and the head of Outward Bound Peacebuilding, who spoke of their enthusiasm for the lifelong foundational relationships they were establishing by discovering the inward knowledge that leads to outward change.

Outward Bound Peacebuilding brings together five Israelis and five Palestinians who are young leaders in their fields—business, religion, and civil society—for a transformational outdoor experience that foster a new way of seeing and understanding their humanness. They learn to know one another in a way that exposes their inner condition, and that they have things to say to one another.

What canst thou say? What canst thou say to witness for peace and for hope? Today you'll use your head knowledge in your lobby visits—and probably some of your heart knowledge, as well as the core conviction in your gut and your bones. You will build relations with staff and lawmakers that will last beyond one visit. You will create power through these relations.

What canst thou say when you return home? Will you share this experience with others? Will you become an agent of peace by building sustained relationships? We are called to both the inward reflection and prayer and the outward action to seek the kingdom of God. This is lifelong work. Many of you have been at it for a long time; for others, this is the start of relationships that will last a lifetime.

Thank you for the opportunity to be with you today. I will conclude my message with a prayer, and then we'll have a period of silence with space for vocal ministry from those present.

Shall we pray our gratitude together?

O Holy One who loves us and creation beyond our wildest imaginings, we thank you—for the opportunity to worship together and for our fellowship. We thank you as we are working for peace and justice, for the opportunity to participate in democracy by asking our elected officials to be accountable for our government's actions, for the gift of using our voices to witness our truths here in Washington and in our home communities, and for the patience to listen deeply and to speak with love.

In October 2013, Diane attended a conversation on poverty with congressional leaders including Rosa DeLauro (CT-03, left) and Lloyd Doggett (TX-35, center).

The Future of Quaker Advocacy

FCNL 2013 Annual Meeting » November 15, 2013 » Washington, DC

Here we are—FCNL at 70 years old: Driven by faith. Grounded in policy. Focused on the future. The future of Quaker advocacy is about you. It is about the lobbying you have done during this annual meeting while you are in Washington, D.C.; the advocacy you will do in the weeks and months ahead when you go back to your homes; and the lobbying FCNL will do for generations to come, long after many of us here are able to walk the halls of Congress.

For over 70 years, FCNL has built relationships here in Washington—on the Hill with members of Congress and their staffs, with our coalition partners, and with Friends and supporters around the country. These relationships span generations. This week, we honored Sen. Jeff Merkley of Oregon with the Edward F. Snyder Award for Disarmament and Peace for his leadership in passing legislation to end the war in Afghanistan. We had quite a bit of back and forth with the senator's office about his schedule, trying to get him to the conference. They were doing their best, but about 10:30 Wednesday evening, my cell phone rang. Since most people know that I am rarely awake after 10:00 p.m., this was unusual.

It was Sen. Merkley calling to find out more about the award. For the next 15 minutes, he recounted the ways he has felt connected to Quakers and to FCNL for over 35 years and his commitment to advancing peace and justice. This relationship started when he was 19 years old, working as an intern for Sen. Mark Hatfield (OR). He made friends with the senator, who was the grandson of Sam and Mariam Levering, the dedicated Friends in Washington who helped found FCNL and devoted themselves to Law of the Sea.

This extended network of connections and other supporters of FCNL that spans generations has become a familiar story I have heard repeatedly in the past two-and-a-half years as I have traveled among Friends. I think of this rich history as a beautifully woven fabric of support that is driven by faith and grounded in policy.

But just how are we focused on the future? In a few minutes, you will hear the stories of six young adults who joined FCNL's staff as program assistants just 12 weeks ago. By the time they leave FCNL in eight months, they will have spent about 4% of their lives with us. And with deference to all the parents in the room who know that the first year of a child's life is the most formative, I'm guessing that for most of the people who come to work as program assistants, the year they spend with FCNL ranks as the second most formative year of their lives—a time when aspirations and dreams intersect with professional and social networking, weaving them into the grounding of peace and justice policymaking.

Last night, Reza Aslan told us how transformative his summer internship with FNCL was 20 years ago. It helped him realize his own path forward in life by introducing him to people who are driven by faith, grounded in policy, and focused on the future.

FCNL's yearlong internship program began in 1970. Over the past 43 years, we have had 176 interns, or as their job title states, program assistants. What began as a trickle—a few years with one, two, or three program assistants—has grown to eight program assistants each year for the past five years.

Young adult engagement at FCNL is more than the year-long internship program. In fact, our program assistants are only one aspect of the future of Quaker advocacy. Let's imagine together what that future might look like. Envision a growing body of (large F) Friends and (small f) friends dedicated to pursuing the world we seek through changing political, cultural, and social institutions.

There will be many younger social justice advocates within this growing movement, who will also be more racially and ethnically diverse than those of us who fill this room.

Many will encounter FCNL in other ways than coming to work in our office for a year, perhaps as volunteers for a summer or a January term or as Spring Lobby Weekend participants. Others may hold a live event on their campus or in their communities or create art or drama that informs, educates, and influences.

They will create a presence for FCNL in new media and in new ways that we haven't yet imagined. The future of Quaker advocacy includes many bright, sophisticated, dedicated individuals who will teach us.

I like to imagine the future of Quaker advocacy also includes a growing number of peace and conflict studies programs on campuses across the country using FCNL as the *go-to* source for information and advocacy on federal peace and justice policies. I can also picture the cadre of young adults who have had a connection with FCNL in some capacity moving into decision-making policy positions in Washington and in state capitols where they will shape policy for peace and justice.

When I think of the future of Quaker advocacy, I see the resurgence of a prophetic witness.

I didn't grow up wanting to be a lobbyist, and I didn't enter middle age wanting to run a Quaker organization. I grew up wanting to be a teacher, and I was. But my religious training and the experiences I had at a young age seeing poverty up close and learning compassion led me to keep asking the deeper questions.

I wonder what the 52 men and women who founded FCNL 70 years ago in Richmond, Indiana, considered would be the life of this organization. Could they have imagined a strong cohort of 35 staff advocating daily on the Hill, coupled with tens of thousands of grassroots lobbyists across the country?

Would they have thought that occupying a prime corner of real estate on Capitol Hill in Washington, D.C., was an effective witness in Washington? Would they have invested resources to assure that younger cohorts of Friends and supporters could carry out this work?

You should know that we are pretty attached to this program and having eight young people working with us every year on disarmament, Middle East peace, the environment, peaceful prevention, immigration, Native American issues, federal budget communications, and Quaker outreach.

But why try to work uphill for peace, justice, and freedom on Capitol Hill at a time when cynicism about the character and operation of government and government officials is widespread and when disillusionment about the church and organized religion is both common and vocal?

I believe it's because religion should be vital and relevant, and the health and future of democracy rest upon responsible participation by informed and concerned citizens. I believe this is the future of Quaker advocacy.

Reimagining U.S. Foreign Policy

Intermountain Yearly Meeting » June 12, 2014 » Ghost Ranch, NM

We are living in a time of enormous change. This is a time when communication across the globe happens in an instant, a time when we recognize the rising economic strength of other countries, a time when the old assumptions and behaviors of the United States are questioned. It is a time that demands a new approach to how the United States will engage in the world.

We are sorely in need of a new foreign policy that is effective and ethical, that turns away from militarism and violent conflict, and that promotes the world we seek—a world free of war and the threat of war, made up of societies with equity and justice for all, that includes communities where every person's potential may be fulfilled, and that restores our earth.

Many of us came to our first Quaker meetings because of the Peace Testimony. We may not have known a lot more about the *peculiar people* known as Friends, but most of us knew that Quakers shun violence and promote peace. What does this mean in action? Are we just another anti-war group with our beautiful blue bumper stickers and yard signs that declare "War Is Not the Answer," or do we have something to say to the world today about peace and what makes for peace? Moreover, how do we live into our vision of the world we seek?

"Shared Security: Reimagining U.S. Foreign Policy" is the joint project created by the American Friends Service Committee (AFSC) and the Friends Committee on National Legislation (FCNL) to offer a perspective about a more effective role for the United States in this changing world. It describes what Friends have to say to the world today about the changes we believe are vital to our world now and for the future.

So, why is now the time to reimagine U.S. Foreign Policy? From Iraq, Afghanistan, our bloated Pentagon budget, and our military in search of a mission, to resource wars driving conflict, globalization, income inequality, technology, cyber warfare, drones, robots, and more, the reasons are seemingly endless.

I would posit that it is increasingly accepted, although not always explicitly stated by policymakers, that the U.S. wars in Iraq and Afghanistan were mistakes. Even military leaders concede that these wars didn't work out. Yet there are still lawmakers who cling to the idea that they voted correctly in approving the billions of dollars we have spent on these wars and who cannot declare that Congress was wrong in approving the 2001 Authorization for Use of Military Force (AUMF). They don't want to acknowledge that soldiers have died in vain, but the fact is that the public's willingness to put boots on the ground has faded.

Last fall when we lobbied against the president's threatened air strikes on Syria for the use of chemical weapons, congressional offices told us that the calls from their constituents ran nine to one against military actions. While a few members of Congress suggested that we ought to be prepared to come to Ukraine's assistance to resist Russian aggression, that idea died quickly in Washington. The public appetite for war has diminished significantly and lawmakers know this.

That hasn't stopped Congress from feeding the beast known as the military industrial complex. However, there is growing public discourse—at least among progressive think tanks—over the wasteful and useless spending on weapons and military contracts that have made

Lockheed Martin, Boeing, General Dynamics, and their colleagues rich and that have made many communities and their people poorer and less safe. Even military pensions and health benefits are under scrutiny, driven by the requirements under sequestration to cut costs at the Pentagon and the unsustainable spending level of these benefits.

Congress resists reducing Pentagon spending for weapons systems that are archaic, citing the value of local jobs even before they are produced. With federal expenditures for the Pentagon at nearly $550 billion annually, we have a long way to go. And with Congress refusing to cut the Overseas Contingency Operations account—the offline appropriation to fund the wars in Iraq and Afghanistan, even as U.S. engagement in those wars ends—we have a long way to go.

The current public opinion against U.S. military engagement hasn't stopped us from deploying U.S. troops in Africa: special ops, support for drone bases and military trainers who are engaged in 100 estimated operations.

Often these are cited as training missions with military or police in the host nation. The public is largely unaware that we still have U.S. military bases in 80 countries, costing taxpayers millions and millions of dollars annually.

Increasingly, we see that violent conflicts in the world are driven by resource wars over water, food, land, and mineral rights. Efforts to control and concentrate power drive conflict.

Syria may be the best example. While the ongoing war in Syria that has killed tens of thousands of people and created sorrowful humanitarian losses is about far more than resources, the policies of Bashar Assad that drove people to farm in lands without water caused significant drought. Subsequently, the migration of huge populations shifted people into communities that also lacked the infrastructure to sustain them.

As Quakers in these challenging times, we often cite the peace testimony from the words of George Fox to "utterly deny all outward wars and strife and fightings."

We have also been moved by the words of Margaret Fell in a 1660 paper delivered to the king and both houses of Parliament:

> *"We are a people that follow after those things that make for peace, love and unity; it is our desire that others' feet may walk in the same, and do deny and bear our testimony against all strife, and wars, and contentions that come from the lusts that war in the members, that war in the soul... and love and desire the good of all."*

As Steve Smith writes in the Pendle Hill pamphlet "Living in Virtue, Declaring Against War," the Peace Testimony was first understood not as a general philosophical principle, but as the expression of changed lives, the fruit of personal spiritual transformation. Perhaps even more significant is the admonition "to live in the virtue and power that takes away the occasion for all war." This is what Friends have to offer that is more than being an anti-war group or a progressive lobbying or service organization.

Our power to live and act does not come from the world's power, political power, or the *empire* model of the national security state. The power that fuels and sustains us comes from the abiding love of the Spirit. The universal experience of binding love that we know in moments of worship and in community with one another draws us to act in the world with love.

We are not alone in this experience; many people of faith and many who profess no faith also act in the world with love. But Quakers, as a religious group, are unique in our persistence of living our faith into the world and striving for peace and justice. This faith in action is not simply a historical legacy of the Religious Society of Friends. Although we can claim a rich history with a deep spirit for change, our call to imagine and live into a world that does justice, pursues peace, and heals our earth is right now.

Fortunately, there are solutions to the old ways that aren't working. "Shared Security" combined the experience of almost 100 years of AFSC's work around the world providing Quaker service in areas of conflict and deprivation with FCNL's 70 years of advocacy on Capitol Hill promoting public policies that build a better world. The working paper outlines the principles and offers some solutions:

1. We should use peaceful means to achieve peaceful ends. That includes civilian leadership in our State Department and the U.S. Agency for International Development (USAID) that is adequately funded and well-equipped in peacebuilding theory and practice. This would include mediation and conflict resolution, transitional justice, sustainable economies, and nonviolent problem solving. It includes a philosophy that we must address the root causes of conflict as well as the symptoms.

2. We should engage in robust diplomacy. At the international level, the current diplomatic engagement with Iran and the P-5 is a particular focus of FCNL right now. We are lobbying to prevent Congress from passing more sanctions and thereby scuttling the current negotiations between the P-5 and Iran for an agreement on Iran's nuclear program. The six-month negotiations that started in January will end on July 20. At our

annual meeting in November, our lobby day will focus on asking Congress to sustain diplomacy with Iran.

3. Effective State Department diplomacy within countries would engage with civil society, building trust and friendship by knowing the language, religion, and culture and by listening to local leaders who comprehend the nation's needs with human rights and rule of law.

4. Security assistance must be reformed to move from training and equipping foreign militaries and police to supporting comprehensive, civilian rule of law and justice systems.

5. Our international institutions and protocols should be strengthened and used to advance true shared security. This includes the United Nations and its agencies. It also includes support and encouragement for building the capacity in diplomacy, violence prevention, and non-military responses of regional organizations such as the African Union, Organization of American States, the Arab League, and the Association of Southeast Nations.

6. The United States should ratify and sign important global treaties, including the Comprehensive Test Ban Treaty, the Mine Ban Treaty, the Arms Trade Treaty, the UN Convention on the Rights of the Child, and the Convention on the Elimination of All Forms of Discrimination Against Women.

7. We should repeal the 2001 Authorization for Use of Military Force (AUMF), the law that has been the justification for the "War on Terror." Passed just after

9/11 with one dissenting vote, this is the law that brought us increasing power of the National Security Agency and the Guantanamo Bay prison and has been cited by the Obama Administration for the use of lethal drones.

The benefits of a more ethical and effective foreign policy are many. It would address the root causes of violent conflict such as climate disruption, resource wars, and corruption. It would proactively promote peace by prioritizing diplomacy and peacebuilding. It would help build systems of justice, rule of law, and human rights. It would promote equality. The United States would no longer be the dominating military power of the globe, consuming disproportionate resources. We would concede the worn-out American exceptionalism cross that we bear.

Reimagining U.S. foreign policy is not only the work of Friends; it is the work of all who long for a more peaceful and just world. However, Quakers today play a vital role in our local communities, with policymakers in Washington, D.C., and in our service around the globe. Just as Quakers throughout history have been led to change injustice and to stand against war, we are called today to follow those things that make for peace, love, and unity.

Before I conclude, I want to share a brief story about a message I heard when worship at Langley Hill Friends Meeting in Virginia a few months ago. A Friend stood fairly early in the hour and said, "I want to encourage everyone to speak up. We have messages to offer and it's important that we can be heard."

My heart began racing as I recognized that this message was exactly what I had been thinking about—that Friends have messages our elected officials need to hear and that we must speak up. We must use our voices. If we won't use our voices to speak our messages to the world, we can't expect that others will.

Alas, I never had the opportunity to extend this message. The hour was filled will rich vocal ministry, spoken in a loud and distinctive fashion. So, I am sharing it today. Friends: Do speak up—not only so that others in our silent meetings might hear you, but so that the world can hear our message of hope.

Meaningful memories and connections being made in Taos, NM.

Perfect Love Casts Out Fear

Jamestown Friends Meeting » November 2, 2014 » Jamestown, NC

Friends, I give thanks to God for this beautiful day, for Jamestown Friends, and for our wider community of the Religious Society of Friends. Today, I am using text from I John 4:18, "There is no fear in love, but perfect love casts out fear; for fear has to do with punishment, and whoever fears has not reached perfection in love."

You might think it unusual that a lobbyist would come to deliver a message about love and fear. Lobbyists typically get cast as *Washington insiders* and are associated with Congress, an institution whose standing among the American public is suffering these days. Many people consider politics a dishonest business, caught in a web of moneyed interests. Whether defense contractors, fossil-fuel or pharmaceutical industries, or any number of trade associations that contribute to their election, the fact is that nonprofits and for-profits alike are *paying to play* in our political system. However, it is still a system that relies on individual voting, which is why so much money is spent to earn your vote.

While we are on the subject, it does matter that you vote, and it matters who gets elected to Congress. I encourage you to vote on Tuesday.

I also encourage you to do more than just vote on Tuesday, as a matter of being a good citizen. I want you to follow and build relationships with your senators and the representatives in your district. I want to challenge you to consider how your willingness to stay engaged with your members of Congress or your state legislators is also a matter of spiritual discipline.

Spiritual disciplines are those actions we take that draw us closer to God—prayer, journal-writing, spiritual reading, fasting, serving others, worshiping in singing and in silence. When we practice getting closer to God, we open our hearts in new ways.

I like to think of the lobbying we do with the Friends Committee on National Legislation (FCNL) as a spiritual discipline. Our communication with elected officials is not just about politics, being right, or winning; it is about carrying a message and a truth and offering ideas that show another way.

Now, I'm guessing that many of you have engaged with your elected officials, and at times that connection or communication may not have felt like you were getting closer to God. Perhaps it may have felt like you were drawing away from God because the member of Congress angered you. A lot about politics can be maddening and make us feel discouraged. We may even harbor some fear about talking to our elected officials, and that fear may emerge from thinking we don't have enough information or know exactly what to say.

There are a couple of ways to deal with that fear:

» Pray and follow your heart.

» Use the information on FCNL's website or in our action alerts.

In our desire to draw closer to God, we open ourselves to how God's love can transform us and transform the world. Our work in this world is not to be the savior, but to use what we have been given and to keep open.

"Love was the first motion, and thence a concern arose to spend some time with the Indians, that I might feel and understand their life and the spirit they live in, if haply I might receive some instruction from them, or they might be in any degree helped forward by my following the leadings of truth among them; and as it pleased the Lord to make way for my going at a time when the troubles of war were increasing, and when, by reason of much wet weather, travelling was more difficult than usual at that season, I looked upon it as a favorable opportunity to season my mind, and to bring me into a nearer sympathy with them.

As mine eye was to the great Father of Mercies, humbly desiring to learn his will concerning me, I was made quiet and content ...."

— John Woolman, 1763

The humility and obedience that John Woolman displays in this brief passage is inspirational. Rather than being afraid of the Indians during a time of war or being put off by the inconvenience of traveling to see them in bad weather, Woolman says he wanted to "understand their life and the spirit they live in." He didn't go to see them because he was angry or self-righteous; he went motivated by love. He provided a presence of love.

These midterm elections have brought a barrage of commercials playing to our fears—that terrorists are at our doorstep, we are at risk of Ebola infections, women will be less than equal, the country is suffering an irreversible decline, etc. Both Republicans and Democrats play these cards using different messages, depending on the party. The challenge of these commercials is that, even after the elections, they pollute our culture with fear.

Media rev up this cycle of fear, even when elections aren't happening. Our multi-channel opportunities for news and information enable us to narrow our intake of information to those who share our political perspective, or we can turn off the news altogether, frustrated by the lack of objectivity or the sense of hopelessness about the multitude of problems facing our world and our communities. In some ways this numbing or indifference may be an even greater risk to our democracy than the divisions.

There was a point this summer when the erupting violence and injustices we witnessed in Gaza and Israel; in Russia and Ukraine; and in Ferguson, Missouri, felt apocalyptic. Coupled with the overarching threat of climate disruption and rising income inequality, it is understandable that we can feel numbed, discouraged, or hopeless.

Yet, there is another way. When I was a teenager coming into an understanding of the power of God's love, my favorite chapter in the Bible was I Corinthians 13, the so-called *love chapter*, because it provides clear guidelines:

> *"[L]ove is patient and kind, love is not jealous or boastful, it is not arrogant or rude, it does not insist on its own ways; love bears all things, hopes all things and endures all things."*

As I got older, I also came to appreciate the last verse of Chapter 12, when Paul writes, "And I will show you still a better way." This set up from Paul's letter to the Corinthians is a something of a *how-to*.

This spirit of love is the basis of our work in this world, Friends. All of you are carrying a ministry that allows you to bear this witness—whether with your family or other Quakers, in your neighborhood, with the people of your community who are poor, or even to the people in your community who are wealthy or powerful.

I believe that our life experiences (our stories) provide important ways that we can speak truth to power, that we can witness to our elected officials about what we believe are the actions our government can take to move us into right relationship with one another and with God.

For FCNL, this motion of love is the basis of our witness for public policies that create a better world. We are driven by faith, based in a God that loves us. We reject the idea that we cannot do anything, and we embrace the idea that we must do what we can.

Because we seek a world free of war and the threat of war, we are asking Congress to make room for diplomacy with Iran and to repeal the 2001 Authorization for Use of Military Force (AUMF). We are pressing lawmakers to cut funding for the B-61 tactical nuclear weapon, and we are promoting new programs for peacebuilding that provide solutions to violent conflict.

Because we seek a society with equity and justice for all, we are pressing for comprehensive immigration reform that includes a path to citizenship. We are advocating for changes to federal drug sentencing that has disproportionately incarcerated African Americans. We stand in support with Native Americans for laws that begin to right the wrongs committed to Indigenous peoples.

Because we seek a community where every person's potential may be fulfilled, we lobby to reduce the amount of funding given to the Pentagon and re-prioritize federal funding to programs that lift people out of poverty, like housing and food assistance. We are lobbying for policy changes that promote a higher minimum wage and extend long-term unemployment benefits.

Because we seek an earth restored, we are calling our members of Congress to support a Call to Conscience—to recognize that they must act to address climate disruption and support mitigation efforts—both in our own country and around the world to save lives.

Thank you for being part of this work through your prayers, your time, your contributions, and your advocacy. I must confess that I have not reached what 1 John describes as "perfection in love," but I do believe that God's perfect love instructs us, holds us, and allows us to act in the world in God's spirit of love.

An FCNL staff photo from 2014.

A Multitude of Troubles

FCNL 2015 Annual Meeting » November 12, 2015 » Washington, DC

There are a multitude of troubles in the world; all manner of ways we are out of right relationship with each other, with our planet, and with God. The brokenness of our world can be heartbreaking as evidenced in the small child who washes ashore in the Mediterranean, one of the hundreds of thousands of refugees fleeing the deadly conflict in Syria; the violence brewing in Burundi; the erosion of civil rights or the anguish of families killed by lethal drone strikes of the U.S. government.

We see this brokenness much closer to home—in the disparity between rich and poor and the lives of people just outside our doors who have no homes and live on the streets, often cycling through shelters, treatment centers, and prisons. Each of these people has a story of love lost, of a life gone awry because of illness, oppression, or just bad luck.

We grieve the brokenness of climate change, watching the erosion of entire villages along coastal lands in Alaska and Micronesia; the erasing of people's livelihoods in the destruction of homes; the forced migration from the debilitating losses of climate disruption.

These troubles burden our hearts and souls. They feed a political life of fear. We can find ourselves afraid, angry, even despondent. We may ask, "What can I do? What is my part? How can we end the violence, heal a broken world, and bring hope to darkness?"

Friend Jim Corbett, one of the founders of the Sanctuary Movement, once wrote, "Individuals can resist injustice, but only in community can we do justice."

When you give voice to injustice, stand to speak when you'd rather be sitting down, overcome your own fear, and speak truth to power, you are doing your part.

That is why you have come to Washington—to use your voice, to counter injustice and build for peace. It is possible for our shared values to influence our government. That is why you are part of the FCNL community: to witness to those who have the authority and power to change laws, asking them to use their power for creating a more peaceful and just world.

You are part of the FCNL community because you know and have seen how restoring right relationships includes building relationships with your members of Congress.

Alice Walker, the brilliant author and poet who has written movingly about injustice and oppression of Black women, said, "The most common way people give up their power is by thinking they don't have any."

You are part of FCNL because we are a community. Our geographical community extends beyond Washington, D.C., to embrace the entire United States of America. It welcomes the 400 of you in the room tonight, and it includes the tens of thousands of people across the country who join us to communicate with lawmakers, to write letters to the editor, to engage in civil discourse with family and friends, and to practice the art of friendly persuasion.

While we are a Quaker-led organization, we are also a network that embraces people of all faiths and those of no established faith. From the earliest days of our history as an organized religious body, Friends confronted governmental authority, petitioning for changes to unfair laws.

Quaker history of the past 350 years is replete with stories of lives that speak. John Woolman's quiet boycott of all materials produced by the hands of slaves, Elizabeth Cady Stanton's organizing for women's suffrage, FCNL's lobby for peace all stem from the inward experience of God and of love that is manifested into outward action.

Quakers have been the guiding force for FCNL since our founding 73 years ago. Discernment from inward reflection to outward action persists in our legislative priority setting as Quaker meetings and churches guide FCNL on our legislative priorities. The living testimonies of the Religious Society of Friends—testimonies of peace, equality, simplicity, integrity, and community—are not only Quaker testimonies. They are values shared by millions of people around the globe. They are certainly shared by those who are part of the FCNL network. We welcome all to be a part of the FCNL community.

Just eight weeks ago, when Pope Francis was headed to Washington, we put a big banner up on FCNL's outside wall that read, "Quakers Welcome Pope Francis." One of my favorite moments of his visit was the few minutes he spent on the outside Portico following his message to the Joint Meeting of Congress.

In that meeting, he had urged Congress to see the common home we all share, to work for the common good. He expressed his confidence in Congress to act justly—a confidence that too many citizens in our own country lack.

He was gentle, yet commanding; humble, yet filled with the authority of love. But it was when he stepped out to talk to the people—those of us assembled on the National Mall—that he captured me completely. There, he asked with deep sincerity that we pray for him, and for those who don't pray to send their good intentions. This humble request is one we can all ask of each other: Pray for me; send me your good intentions.

I was thrilled to have Pope Francis deliver those words before Congress and name the justice we seek. He called for the elimination of the death penalty and for an end to small arms trade that fuels deadly conflict. His presence and the careful attention he commanded reinforced deeply for me the essential role we play in delivering our messages to Congress.

It was exciting to see members of Congress respond to Pope Francis, but it is not only his voice or the voice of religious leaders who must call on Congress to build the structures for peace and justice. It will require tens of thousands of voices doing their part. We are called to live out our convictions through love made visible. We are called to be bold for the world we seek.

With your help, we have taken bold steps to strengthen our lobby for peace and justice. We are changing, not in the essence of who we are as a Quaker lobby working for peace and justice, but in breadth and depth. I came to lead an organization standing on the shoulders of giants—E. Raymond Wilson, Ed Snyder, and Joe Volk.

I came to an organization that had been carefully stewarded by its General Committee, an organization that asked people to build the ladder of engagement with lawmakers and that had a strong presence on Capitol Hill that has been cultivated over decades of sustained and careful policy analysis and legislative advocacy.

The intentions this organization set forth 10 years ago with the Futures Working Group to engage more young adults have become real. The current capital campaign, "The World We Seek: Now Is the Time," has allowed us to design and develop new programs and strengthen others that have been part of FCNL for many years. FCNL is building from this solid foundation to become an even stronger lobbying operation in four ways.

First, it is vital for us to support the next generation of advocates. We see what happens when young adults talk to members of Congress. Legislators listen. Their demeanors change, and they pay attention to these new voices. Cultivating leadership for social justice advocacy is the goal of our Young Adult programs.

The young adults who connect to FCNL bring their passion to address the brokenness they see in our world—whether that is climate change or immigration, mass incarceration or deadly conflict. Our role at FCNL is to train on how to be politically engaged in effective ways that build right relationships. We provide opportunities for leadership in social justice advocacy.

We are also building out our lobbying and strengthening our community with young adults in other ways. Ten years ago, FCNL began a Spring Lobby Weekend, thanks to our friends at Wilmington College. Last year, we welcomed 182 young adults from across the country who joined us in asking their members of Congress to support a moral call to conscience.

This year, we established the Advocacy Corps, a 10-month program that pays young adults ages 19 to 30 to organize their local community around federal legislation. After taking part in a week-long immersive training in community organizing, media outreach, and lobbying, they commit to working 25 hours per month mobilizing their communities to lobby members of Congress to advance big, long-term change.

We are also connecting across generations by reconnecting our alumni—the interns, program assistants, and young fellows who have worked at FCNL over the past 40 years—to give advice or assistance to current young fellows when they leave FCNL to advance in their careers.

Significantly, this capital campaign is creating an endowment of $6 million for FCNL's work with young adults. The endowment assures that our young adult programs will have sufficient resources to operate in the years to come.

The dedication of our General Committee to financial stewardship for the future gives us the confidence to be bold in reaching out widely to engage more people in the FCNL community. Through our Young Adult program, we can create a more visible presence on Capitol Hill.

We see how our network of advocates makes a difference. From Iran diplomacy and climate change to police militarization, FCNL's analysis and education lead and inspire others to bring their voices to Washington. Our Quaker Public Policy Institute/Annual Meeting in November and Spring Lobby Weekend in March bring hundreds of people to Capitol Hill to lobby every year. Many return home and lobby their lawmakers in-district.

Not everyone can make it to these two big events, but they still want to lobby with FCNL when they come to Washington, and we want them to lobby. That is why, as part of the capital campaign, we are creating a Quaker Welcome Center in the building adjacent to FCNL's office. This new Welcome Center will be a place we come together in community, provide information on the issues and on how to lobby.

For families traveling to Washington as tourists or for those coming to the Capitol for business, we want visitors to take an extra couple of hours and visit with their members of Congress about legislation FCNL is lobbying on.

The first floor at 205 C Street will offer a meeting room for small gatherings and give another space for welcoming all who wish to lobby with us. The space will be used for committee meetings and coalition meetings. It will include a living room-style space for conversations that benefit from a less formal setting. It will be a place for quiet conversations, perhaps between people who need an *off-line* place to sit together; a place to calm the rhetoric.

And, like the FCNL office building, which turned 10 this year, 205 C Street will also be a green building upon completion. Sustainability is an essential part of who we are. Lobbying for solutions to climate change and holding the vision of an earth restored is evidenced in the commitment we made in our last capital campaign to developing a green building.

Through the careful selection of materials, furnishings, and lighting and using virtual net metering, we are committed to creating a net-zero carbon building. We are dedicated to doing all we can to reduce FCNL's carbon footprint and recognize new best practices to make our existing building as energy efficient as possible.

The second and third floors of the building will be residential. One of the four apartments will be reserved for the Friend in Washington. This historic program has brought scores of Friends to Washington to work with FCNL on a temporary basis.

Now, we will provide a home for those Friends who sojourn with us, offering a one-bedroom apartment while they work in our office and volunteer their time and expertise on a policy issue or priority to FCNL. This program is yet another way to do more policy and advocacy for the world we seek, tapping into the wisdom and experience of seasoned Friends who have much to give.

While I believe each of these areas—the Young Adult work, the Quaker Welcome Center, and the Friend in Washington—makes FCNL a stronger organization through new people and new ways that we are communicating with members of Congress, the capital campaign is also investing in FCNL lobbying. We have seen what working together can achieve; that is, the strong presence of Washington, D.C., lobbyists, coupled with vibrant grassroots. That dynamic work will continue to grow.

The next 18 months of the life of our capital campaign—the public phase—will bring new opportunities to build this community and enhance our critical advocacy for peace and justice. For decades, you have been asked to lobby and

A Multitude of Troubles

you've come through. You have been asked to contribute to the annual fund and you've come through. You have been asked to guide your meeting or church through legislative priorities and you've come through. We thank you, as these actions are essential to our foundation.

But tonight, I'm asking for something more. Starting in January, we will take our organization on the road. From January 2016 to June 2017, we need your help making the FCNL capital campaign events successful. We will be visiting 24 cities, and we will be in eight retirement communities. It's possible that you might live in or close to one of those cities or retirement communities or you might know someone who does.

You are all invited to attend; I'm looking forward to seeing every one of you there. But I encourage you to bring friends, neighbors, and family as well. You are the most effective messengers about the work of FCNL in your local communities. These events will give Friends an understanding of the important work FCNL is doing right now, as well as our plans.

Most importantly, we will invite people to join us and tell them how they can use their voices to be bold and make change in Washington. These will be inclusive events—not only for those who make financial contributions, and not only for those who are already active.

We hope donors and grassroots lobbyists will be in attendance, but these FCNL-on-the-road events will be most successful when new people who don't yet know us participate.

Also, for those of you who are members of a Quaker meeting or church, we ask that you introduce the capital campaign to your meeting.

More and more people—Quakers and others—are being drawn to our effective practice of engaging our nation's leaders. The capital campaign is making it possible for greater participation in civil dialogue on the life and death issues for humanity and our planet. We are boldly leading the way for our policymakers to act for peace and justice.

It is our vision and hope that through our actions, we will continue to create a world free from war, a society with equity and justice for all, a community where every person's potential may be fulfilled, and an earth restored.

Diane meets with Senator Dick Durbin (IL), then Senate Majority Whip, to present him with the 2015 Edward F. Snyder Peace Award.

What We Need Is Here

Dwight and Ardis Michener Lecture, Southeastern Yearly Meeting
January 17, 2016 » Orlando, FL

"Geese appear high over us,
pass, and the sky closes. Abandon,
as in love or sleep, holds
them to their way, clear
in the ancient faith: what we need is here.
And we pray, not
for new earth or heaven,
but to be quiet in heart, and in eye,
clear. What we need is here."

— "What We Need Is Here," by Wendell Barry

I have three core messages about living a life that is both spiritual and political that I will return to throughout this talk, while I share stories of the work we are doing—the collective *we* as Friends and the collective *we* of the Friends Committee on National Legislation (FCNL), that includes Friends and many others around the country who share the vision of the world we seek.

I'll give special emphasis to the work of sustainability because I know that is a particular focus of Southeastern Yearly Meeting, but I will also talk about other priorities that Friends have asked FCNL to address in our lobbying on Capitol Hill.

First, here are some things I believe:

» God's love is sufficient.

» Our spiritual lives are integral in every aspect of our beings, including our political lives. This undivided life calls us.

» The wholeness of Friends' faith and practice is needed now more than ever in the political life of our country. God's love is sufficient. We are covered by God's love.

In September 2001, I was living in West Hartford, Connecticut, working for a lobbying firm in Hartford, the state capital. My work focused on policies to end homelessness through making more affordable and supportive housing available. My two daughters were in elementary school, my son was in his second year of college in New York City, and my husband was writing for the Hartford Courant.

The morning of 9/11 was a stunningly beautiful New England day—brilliant blue sky with a few white clouds, warm sun, no humidity. When I walked in the office that morning, my colleague shared the news of the first airplane that had crashed into the World Trade Center. Then came the second and the third and the fourth. I was meeting a colleague midway between Hartford and Boston and listened as the news coverage tried to make sense of what happened.

We can probably all tell a story of where we were and how we responded when we heard this news—shock, disbelief, confusion. It took several hours for me to contact my son, who was physically safe. My husband picked up our daughters at school; we were relieved to be together at home, and we were grateful that our Worship and Ministry called a meeting for worship that evening.

In that epochal moment of tragedy, immediate grief, and the deep knowledge that life as we know it would be affected, the place I wanted to be was with Friends in my community of faith. I don't recall the specific vocal ministry of that gathering, but it was a covered meeting for me. It was covered by God's love.

The certainty of God's presence in the face of not knowing what to do—how to respond, what to think, how to react— was not only comforting; it grounded me. It renewed my faith in a God of love. It helped me begin to make sense of the evil men do. This certain knowledge that God's love is sufficient inhabits my life.

Knowing that there is nothing that can separate us from God's love changes everything. What we need is here. When I have these transcendent moments of truth, I recognize that they rise from the base of teachings, experiences, and attention to the stirring in my soul over a lifetime. The basis of my certainty of God's sustaining love that day in the face of tragedy and confusion comes from the words of Jesus from the Sermon on the Mount:

> *"Therefore I tell you, do not worry about your life, what you will eat or drink; or about your body, what you will wear. Is not life more than food, and the body more than clothes? Look at the birds of the air; they do not sow or reap or store away in barns, and yet your heavenly Father feeds them. Are you not much more valuable than they? Can any one of you by worrying add a single hour to your life? And why do you worry about clothes? See how the flowers of the field grow. They do not labor or spin. Yet I tell you that not even Solomon in all his splendor was dressed like one of these.*

> *"If that is how God clothes the grass of the field, which is here today and tomorrow is thrown into the fire, will he not much more clothe you—you of little faith? So do not worry, saying, 'What shall we eat?' or 'What shall we drink?' or 'What shall we wear?' For the pagans run after all these things, and your heavenly Father knows that you need them. But seek first his kingdom and his righteousness, and all these things will be given to you as well. Therefore do not worry about tomorrow, for tomorrow will worry about itself. Each day has enough trouble of its own."*

> — *Matthew 6:25-34*

At FNCL, we seek a world free of war and the threat of war; we seek a society with equity and justice for all; we seek a community where each person's potential may be fulfilled; and we seek an earth restored. We seek the kingdom of God.

The teaching from the Sermon on the Mount makes it clear that seeking the kingdom of God doesn't happen with our worry or our fear. God's love is sufficient to cover us from our worries and fears. Seeking the kingdom of God is loving God with all our heart, mind, and soul and loving our neighbor as ourselves.

Holding in our hearts this truth that God's love is sufficient is not easy in our society, which is rife with fear. You can name the despair, anger, hopelessness, and cynicism that you may yourselves feel and certainly that we see in others around us. The fear response and the concurrent negative emotions are normal human reactions to economic insecurity, racial injustice, random shooting sprees, extremist violence, war, inhumane treatment of migrants and refugees, and the global imperative of a warming planet.

These conditions, dangers, worries, concerns, fears, sense of abandonment, and loss can also inhabit our lives. We know the brokenness and distance of our society from the kingdom of God. We also know—because of the work for peace, for justice, for an earth restored that we do and that we see others do—that hope is alive and well. The way we live, the choices we make, the actions we can and do take build the world we seek.

There are solutions to the entrenched systems of militarization, racial and economic inequality, and climate change. The solutions come through changing the systems that perpetuate the problems. One important method we have for changing those systems is in our political lives.

Despite the irritation you may feel about political candidates who pander to fear and despite the frustration you may have for the media/entertainment industry that fuels the rhetoric of fear, I encourage you to bring your spiritual selves to politics.

Bring the certain knowledge that God's love is not only sufficient to cover these fears, but that God's love is abundant. Bring your hope that is fostered through the dedicated worship we share; the time of contemplation when we make ourselves open to continuing revelation and discerning God's call for us in this broken yet beautiful world.

This undivided life calls us to live life whole. Our spiritual lives are integral in every aspect of our beings, including our political lives.

One of the reasons I cherish being a Quaker is the acceptance and expectation that my inward life will be reflected in the way I live outwardly. Knowing that God's love covers us gives us the grace to make mistakes. It allows us to stretch, to take risks that we might not otherwise take. As Elizabeth Fry said, "I look not to myself, but to that within me that has to my admiration proved to be my present help and enabled me to do what I believe of myself I could not have done."

This is what Friend Parker Palmer says in his book *Healing the Heart of Democracy*:

"For those of us who want to see democracy survive and thrive—and we are legion—the heart is where everything begins: that grounded place in each of us where we can overcome fear, rediscover that we are members of one another, and embrace the conflicts that threaten democracy as openings to new life for us and for our nation."

Living an undivided life means that we recognize that the vexing problems of violence, climate disruption, and inequality are the problems of "we the people," not just our elected officials.

If we are not engaged with our members of Congress, city council, or state legislators to work with them to solve these difficult problems, we have stepped away from the opportunity to make our society more peaceful, more equal, and sustainable. Living an undivided life calls us to deep civic engagement—beyond voting and volunteering; it is about building relationships.

Living an undivided life means building a bridge between our source of integrity and who we are in the world. It is being fully present in the world as a spiritual person. Living an undivided life is a spiritual quest. It is the quest for simplicity—to be truthful in how we respond to the world around us. When we engage in action that flows from our inner condition, we can act with a kind of courage and compassion. What we need is here.

One of the joys of working at FCNL is listening to the "aha" moments that happen when ordinary citizens, everyday Quakers, walk into the offices of their members of Congress to lobby. Particularly, for people who lobby for the first time, the recognition that there are staff who will listen, or when a delegation of Friends has a sit-down meeting with the senator or representative directly, can be a transformative experience in which the idea of representative democracy comes alive. It is a moment when we are speaking from our authentic selves.

Twice a year, FCNL hosts big events when we encourage Friends to come to Washington to lobby on legislative priorities. I invite you to join us for these events. In November, we held our Quaker Public Policy Institute in conjunction with our Annual Meeting. Two months ago, we had about 350 people join us as part of the FCNL network talking on Capitol Hill about peacebuilding.

Our specific ask was for support of a bill to build U.S. governmental structures for the prevention of violent conflict. Our lobbyists have been working with the Senate Foreign Relations Committee, and specifically with Sen. Ben Cardin's (MD) staff, to introduce a bill to authorize the Atrocities Prevention Board and funding for conflict prevention accounts that the U.S. State Department and U.S. Agency for International Development (USAID) use.

When our staff lobby on the Hill, we are strategic about who we focus on—particularly in the initial stages of seeking co-sponsors for a piece of legislation. When grassroots constituents come to Washington to talk to their members of Congress or visit them in their district offices, FCNL has the opportunity to talk to many more members of Congress— and not just the ones we think we will be champions for a piece of legislation. The fact is that you, as constituents, can be great lobbyists, and you can be most effective with the people you can vote for.

At our Lobby Day in November, when one of the delegations met with their politically conservative senator's staff, they were quite surprised to hear the staff indicate a strong interest in the bill and an appetite to get the senator to cosponsor it. This is because preventing violent conflict is humanitarian, ethical, and financially prudent.

The great story here is that not only were these citizen advocates very effective, but then when Theo and Allyson, who do our lobbying on peacebuilding, were putting together the list of likely co-sponsors, this senator's name was not on it. The meeting the constituents had in this senator's office moved the senator to be a co-sponsor, creating bipartisan support for an important step in preventing deadly conflict.

If we can look beyond the rhetoric and see the people who hold public office as human beings committed to public service, we will find something to like about them, even if we don't like the way they vote or everything they say. When we approach political candidates or elected officials and first see that of God in them, we may see a new opening for dialogue.

Another event FCNL hosts each spring is focused on engaging young adults to lobby and to experience how their voices and stories can help advance peace and social justice. This year's Spring Lobby Weekend will address mass incarceration. We are supporting a bipartisan bill that makes progress in sentencing reform for federal offenses.

This bill, now moving through the Senate with a companion bill in the House, is only a small step in the big effort it will take to change our system of mass incarceration, one that will require states, as well as the federal government, to act.

We recruit widely at colleges and through social media for participation in this Spring Lobby Weekend that spans three intense days in Washington, providing content knowledge from experts on the issue, background on the political dynamics from Hill staff, and training on how to lobby from our own staff.

We are particularly keen to have young adult Friends participate, and we encourage Southeastern Yearly Meeting and your monthly meetings to support the young adults in your meetings to participate.

The surprise and delight from the young people who come to lobby give new meaning to the civics lessons they learned in high school as they understand how to petition the congressional offices that represent them. Young adults demand authenticity and approach their lobbying work with a focused and respectful attitude that inevitably grabs the attention of lawmakers.

Emily Wirzba, our sustainable energy, and environment lobbyist, told me a story about lobbying at Spring Lobby Weekend. She joined Earlham College student Treston Owens from Miami on a member-level visit with Rep. Ileana Ros-Lehtinen (FL-27). Emily shared this:

> *"Rep. Ros-Lehtinen didn't have time to meet with us in her office, so her environmental staffer Wes escorted Treston and me underground through the Capitol building to meet with her in-between votes. We walked right past Nancy Pelosi into the cloak room. Ros-Lehtinen came out, spoke to us for a few minutes, and we handed her a copy of the Gibson resolution. This enabled us to follow up with her*

staffer Wes, and months later, Ros-Lehtinen signed onto the Gibson resolution (after a very broad, collaborative effort with many organizations helping). However, she claimed it was the first time she had seen the resolution, and it really energized Treston to get that experience inside the Capitol building! It was his first time to D.C."

It is a joy to watch young adults like Treston discover how they can express their yearnings for justice and for a sustainable planet to elected officials who can make systemic change. Many of the young adults are committed social change activists; they are the organizers on campus, and they may volunteer in electoral politics.

Others come to Spring Lobby Weekend as part of a college government class, but they all leave with a new sense of their own agency to influence change. They leave us and the congressional offices they visit with hope.

Another way we see young adults integrating their inward condition into their outward actions is through FCNL's Advocacy Corps, a group of 16 young people who organize in their local communities to raise the issue of climate change, focused on asking their members of Congress to take meaningful action. It's been great to have Michelle Lamm of Tallahassee Monthly Meeting as one of the inaugural members of this new program.

Advocacy Corps members design strategies for how they will reach their members of Congress to request action on climate. In addition to getting letters to the editor published in local papers, Michelle took the innovative step of having children in the meeting's First Day School send Christmas cards to Florida's senators, Bill Nelson and Marco Rubio. There are many ways to build relationships with members of Congress!

I want to step back here and take a wider-angle view of political life. At FCNL, we are focused on Washington policy and politics, but the fact is that for all of us our political lives are much bigger than what happens at the national level. We live in a country, in cities, and in towns that are governed by elected officials. So, whether we participate or not in electoral politics, we are governed by the decisions of those we elect.

Friends exhibit extraordinary participation in civic and community life—from serving on neighborhood associations and volunteering in soup kitchens to organizing weekly vigils, these ways of giving our time make our communities stronger and build social cohesion. This social cohesion is the fabric of a rich political life, especially when we interact with those who hold different views and values than we hold.

I see countless ways that Friends provide service, but I also know that Friends often look at the upstream causes of problems and put themselves in the forefront of new ideas, willing to be pioneers or to be in the center of conflict.

Who do you look to as the "patterns, examples of walking cheerfully over the earth, speaking to that of God in everyone we meet?" I have been inspired by the Friends in the meeting that nurtured me—Hartford Meeting in Connecticut. I have watched how Friends who lived in suburban households found ways to lower their carbon footprint and care for the earth: composting (even 25 years ago); eating from their gardens; buying from local farmers; favoring recycled stores over shopping malls; moving from a two-car household to a one-car, energy efficient household and often leaving that car parked to favor biking.

These friends were turning the thermostat down in the winter and up in the summer, installing solar panels, changing to energy efficient light bulbs, and giving up air travel. Seeing the Friends in my community adjust their lives to reduce carbon output makes me realize I can make the same changes.

I am always learning new ways that Quakers let their lives speak. Last summer, I visited Friends in Santa Rosa, California, where there is a vibrant Friends House Retirement Community and a group of folks who have been strong FCNL supporters. The state had been in a drought and restaurants had stopped the practice of bringing water to the table unless requested. It had the effect of making me relish the refreshment of that water, and I felt compelled to drink every drop.

But the new element of conservation that captured me was the Friends who explained how they were collecting the grey water from their own brief showers to reuse for toilet flushing. I got new ideas of how I could reuse and recycle and was prompted to contemplate how our world changes when fresh water is not readily available.

Another story of how Friends are witnessing to care for God's creation is that of Winchester Friends Church in Indiana. I had the pleasure of delivering the Sunday message in the programmed worship at Winchester Friends Church a couple of years ago. The church has a remarkable food bank program that recently expanded to meet the needs of the people who are food insecure in this rural and small-town community. Winchester Friends Church recently completed installation of a 32-panel solar array on top of their meetinghouse annex through a grant funded by Hoosier Interfaith Power and Light.

These are not partisan political actions, but they are political actions because they help shape our political and economic life. We can witness in countless ways.

At FCNL, our office is also a testimony to sustainability on Capitol Hill. This past summer, we celebrated 10 years in our *green building*. Our renovated office building was the first LEED-certified building on Capitol Hill in Washington, D.C. From the geothermal heating/cooling system, bamboo floors, and green roof, to the furnishings made of recycled materials and the ample bike parking, FCNL is a witness for our practice of seeking "an earth restored."

Joe Volk, my predecessor as executive secretary of FCNL, tells the story of Rep. Joe Wilson of South Carolina who visited the FCNL office shortly after it was renovated. As Joe gave the congressman a tour of the building, Rep. Wilson noted the bamboo floors and compelled his aide to make a note—growing bamboo in South Carolina could be an economic development opportunity in his state.

Later this year, we'll begin the renovation of the residential building immediately next door to the FCNL office building. We will create a Quaker Welcome Center on the first floor

What We Need is Here

and reserve one of the four apartments in the building for our Friend in Washington program. Most exciting, we have committed to making this a carbon-neutral building.

Why does this matter as a witness? On a postage-stamp size urban footprint directly across from the Senate office buildings, we see thousands of people passing by our building and scores of people visiting our central location. Friends across the country who are visiting Washington, D.C., stop by for a tour; Friends who participate in our Quaker Public Policy Institute or our Young Adult Spring Lobby Weekend are in and out of the building.

Daily, we host many coalition meetings with our faith-based partners, like the groups who are working together for accountability and transparency of the lethal drones program or as allies with Native American groups in their advocacy or with our partners at Citizens Climate Lobby and the Evangelical Environmental Network.

We offer hospitality and often our staff provides leadership for these coalitions or for leading school groups on lobby visits. One of my favorite stories about young lobbyists is when a small group of Haverford Middle School students came to lobby Rep. Meehan (PA-07) on climate change.

Emily accompanied this small group that had a lively exchange with their member of Congress, who did sign onto the Gibson resolution, a Republican-led resolution that states climate change is real, is caused by humans, and requires action. This important visit by these young lobbyists helped lead to Rep. Meehan's co-sponsorship of this important step.

These individual and organizational efforts to address global warming encourage us to see how our connections and our own actions link us to the wider global community. We know that these individual witnesses are insufficient to the crisis at hand. We also know that it is our elected officials, specifically the U.S. Congress, that is the roadblock to systemic action. Congressional action alone will not fix the problem of climate change, but without congressional action, the effort is much, much more difficult.

As Thomas Merton once said,

> *"The wholeness of Friends' faith and practice is needed now more than ever in our political life. [Our] basic problem is not political; it is apolitical and human. One of the most important things to do is to keep cutting deliberately through political lines and barriers and emphasizing the fact that these are largely fabrications and that there is another dimension, a genuine reality, totally opposed to the fictions of politics: the human dimension which politics pretend to arrogate entirely to themselves. This is the necessary first step along the long way toward the perhaps impossible task of purifying, humanizing, and somehow illuminating politics themselves."*

This statement encourages us to step beyond the lines drawn in culture and politics and see that what is called for is humanizing our political life. We do that by putting ourselves into it.

Friends' voices are needed—not to inflame partisan rhetoric and not to overreact to extreme behavior, but to speak and act on the truth that we know. Our elected officials need and want constituents who will encourage, teach, appreciate, and hold them accountable to work for the common good. They are human, and like all of us, they listen to people around them: people they have relationships with. Developing relationships with those with whom we disagree, or those we would expect more of, can be a spiritual exercise.

Faith communities, as nonpartisan actors, are well-suited to establish the moral foundation for the issues we care about, such as climate change. People of faith care for creation; we express concern for the poor and feel responsible for the wellbeing of future generations.

Faith-based approaches to contentious issues can soften the divisiveness in the national and political culture through respectful interactions, carrying values of partnership, redemption, hope, and a shared future. By recognizing the Light within each individual, people of faith can bring together many to work in a nonpartisan fashion for a thriving future and earth restored.

How do our lives speak? How do we fit in the living stream of the witness of the Religious Society of Friends? What are the specific practices that put Friends in an important role to act?

Many of these practices are conducted by people of all faiths or by people who profess no faith. I don't mean to suggest that Friends alone will change political life or that people who act from a place of religious faith have all the answers.

Much of our work at FCNL is done in collaboration with other faith-based organizations that lobby in Washington, and we also work with others who share our values and goals but profess no specific faith.

I believe there is a clear hunger for the moral and ethical perspective of policy issues, and we can help provide that perspective. During the debate of the Budget Control Act a couple of years ago, I was invited to a meeting convened by Rep. Steny Hoyer of Maryland, a leader in the Democratic caucus, with a small group of faith leaders and about 15 members of Congress.

In the hour-long discussion, those members told us directly how important it was for them to hear from the religious communities in their districts. Constituents who provided stories on how the SNAP food program or housing vouchers or the EITC prevented families from falling more deeply into poverty give these lawmakers information as well as the backing that supports them.

Friends bring important values and practices to political life. Our waiting worship and discernment result in unity of purpose. We labor together on concerns, and when we reach clearness, our forward direction can be powerful. The statements that come from this work together— usually in the form of a minute; sometimes an epistle; or for organization, a joint statement—give a unified grounding to work from. In political parlance, we are establishing a base of support.

I want to name some of these statements that have guided FCNL's work on climate change.

What We Need is Here

First, there's the Moral Call to Conscience. Bipartisan Congressional action is vital to catalyze the necessary national and global solutions to climate disruption.

FCNL's Call to Conscience on Climate Disruption seeks a bipartisan group of congressional representatives to publicly declare that climate disruption is real, is primarily caused by human activities, and is inflicting great harm on present and future generations and our beloved Earth. We are pleased that after working for years on this strategy, we have begun to see a change in the dialogue in Congress on climate change.

There was also the Kabarak Call for Peace and Ecojustice that was approved at the Sixth World Gathering of Friends World Committee for Consultation at Kabarak University in Nakuru, Kenya, in 2012. I was in the worship session at the World Gathering when this Call was approved. Those who had labored in creating the Call had not expected the ease with which Way opened to affirm our unity.

Next, Facing the Challenge of Climate Change, a shared statement by Quaker groups—Quaker EarthCare Witness, the Quaker United Nations Office, FCNL, and the Friends World Committee for Consultation (FWCC)—was developed in September 2014 in conjunction with the Peoples' Climate March. It has since been updated and signed by scores of Quaker meetings and organizations.

The statement read, "We call on our leaders to make the radical decisions needed to create a fair, sufficient, and effective international climate change agreement. As Quakers, we understand anthropogenic climate change (climate change due to human activities) to be a symptom of a greater challenge; how to live sustainably and justly on this Earth."

While not a Quaker document, the power of *Laudato Si*, the Papal encyclical issued in June 2015 offers a framework that is both universal and Roman Catholic. There is much in this teaching document that Friends will find compelling. Pope Francis calls on us to act to reverse climate change for the people of the world, particularly those who are poor and directly affected; for the peace of the world, knowing that climate disruption drives conflict and migration; and for the planet, God's creation. It is a beautiful spiritual reading; I commend it to you.

Our commitment to community seeks to build relationships across hard divides. We have seen throughout the history of Friends faith and practice the understanding that our common humanity is greater than the divisions we create by nationality or religion or race or political perspectives. We believe it is essential to lobby with every member of Congress because there is that of God in every member of Congress, in their staff people, and in ourselves.

We have the ability to live with the "fierce urgency of now" while understanding our place in God's time. One of the ways that FCNL keeps its faithfulness as a Quaker organization is through our governing body, the General Committee, and through robust participation in our legislative priorities and policy setting process.

Our General Committee is a board of nearly 200 Quakers from around the country who represent yearly meetings,

Friends' organizations, perspectives, and theological traditions within the Religious Society of Friends. The General Committee determines FCNL's legislative agenda based on our overall policy statement: The World We Seek.

FCNL seeks to bring spiritual values and Friends' testimonies to bear on public policy decisions. Our legislative priorities arise from a process of worshipful discernment, carried out by Friends in hundreds of Quaker meetings and churches across the country every two years. We solicit the views and concerns of Quaker meetings, churches, and organizations around the country that led our committee to discern the following priorities for our lobbying and public education work during the 114th Congress (2015–2016):

» Advance peacebuilding and the peaceful prevention and resolution of violent conflict.

» Reduce military spending and militarized responses to global and domestic situations.

» Promote nuclear disarmament and non-proliferation.

» Support solutions to mitigate and adapt to climate disruption.

» Reduce the influence of money in politics.

» Address poverty, reduce income inequality, and promote economic justice.

» Advance policies that reduce mass incarceration.

» Continue our witness and advocacy on Native American issues.

» Promote fair, humane, and demilitarized immigration policies.

At the staff level, we also consider legislative opportunities, specific expertise, leadings, and available resources. Our policy statement, The World We Seek, gives FCNL the flexibility to respond to crises and to other important legislative opportunities as Way opens. The General Committee calls upon its members and welcomes other Friends and like-minded people to work on these priorities.

Many other deeply held concerns will continue to receive attention from individual Friends, monthly meetings and churches, yearly meetings, and other Quaker organizations. Working together to find solutions to complex problems, we find our spiritual experience deepening as we seek divine guidance, ask for renewed strength and act with hope.

Every two years, we ask local meetings to discern the priorities that arise from meetings and churches. I hope you will participate in this priority setting process by responding in the next three months. FCNL needs your guidance. More than that, however, I hope you will respond because it is an opportunity for your monthly meeting to consider the concerns of your own contemplative practice. For the meeting this can be a spiritual exercise.

At FCNL, we see our work as both prophetic and pragmatic—prophetic in working for the world we seek; pragmatic in taking the steps we can right now to move toward the world we seek.

What We Need is Here

Here are some pragmatic steps we can do together this year and next year for "an earth restored."

» Thank members of Congress who have co-sponsored the Gibson resolution.

» Work with FCNL and others in your community to ask these legislators to support the Gibson resolution.

» Advocate for meaningful bipartisan legislative solutions to climate change, with a particular focus on a non-regressive price on carbon.

We have been monitoring proposals and discussion of carbon tax bills. We expect that these conversations will accelerate in Washington—although perhaps not publicly—through the course of this year in anticipation of a new administration in 2017. Putting a price on carbon will require bipartisan leadership. We will work to assure that such a tax will not be harmful to low-income households.

The Paris Climate Conference last December was significant in advancing global progress to address climate change with the commitment from nearly 200 countries who brought their countries plans to the conference. Secretary Kerry announced at the Climate Conference a pledge of $800 million to climate finance from the United States.

This investment and that from other wealthy nations is essential for mitigation and adaptation in poor nations that have been hardest hit by global warming. The expectation is that the Green Climate Fund will need to ratchet up the commitment to $100 Billion by 2020. We will also continue to monitor opportunities to spur investment and incentives for renewable energy.

Partnerships are essential to advancing our advocacy. Some of the groups we work with regularly include other faith groups, business groups, military, conservation organizations, environmental organizations, and climate justice leaders. I encourage you to think of others in your own communities with whom you can partner in talking to your lawmakers. A bigger base of support is a strong motivator for lawmakers.

I will end with words of encouragement to you for living an undivided life and integrating our spiritual and political lives from Joey Hartmann-Dow, another member of the Advocacy Corps. Joey writes eloquently in Friends Journal about how she has learned to use her own story in legislative advocacy.

"What I intend to present now is a new confidence in my voice as a citizen, and to act on my responsibility to that role. I am inspired by the people who work within and with the system: the congressional staffers I've met, the activists, and the people who continue to share their stories.

I encourage anyone and everyone to take part in the process in whatever way you can, whether that's committing to a lifestyle that reflects your values, meeting with your representatives and senators, or purposely engaging in conversations about climate action. I'm so grateful I learned to value my significance as one part of this story; now I can't wait to see what happens when members of communities come together to bring their voices to our elected leaders, so they can move forward with the support of their constituents.

We are in this together, and through human connection we will recognize our common needs as residents of the same planet. Maybe seeing our communities, nation, political system, and earth as interconnected parts will help us see the urgent value in an earth restored. And maybe your story could be the beginning of a conversation that will change the world."

What we need is here.

As mentioned in the previous speech, FCNL was deep in construction on the Quaker Welcome Center in 2016. Photos by Jennifer Domenick/FCNL.

Photo by Joe Molieri/FCNL

From Despair to Strength and Joy

North Pacific Yearly Meeting » July 14, 2016 » Spokane, WA

"Peace I leave with you. My peace I give unto you. Not as the world giveth, give I unto you. Let not your heart be troubled, neither let it be afraid." John 14:27

What is your condition today? Is it despairing? Is it hopeful? Is it peaceful? Is it joyful? Perhaps you, like many of us, move from one feeling to another, depending on your social media feed.

What's on Facebook? What's on Twitter? Or perhaps it's based on a newspaper article or television show you may have watched recently. I know there are at least a couple of people in this room who have just come from the FGC

Gathering with 1,000 other Friends. And you may be feeling blissful, full of emotion, and a spiritual deepening from being with Friends.

On the other hand, violence, cruelty, injustice, unrest, and inaction to address climate disruption are issues that can make us despair. Our frustrations can often include fear and disappointment with our political and elected officials. In times of despair, it's easy to move through these negative emotions.

Today, I want to tell you a little bit about how about my work at FCNL brings me hope. I also want to tell you that the trajectory from despair to strength and joy is not a straight line or even a beautiful arc, but it is possible. And these emotions can live together within us. I want to challenge you to see that, through our lives in the Spirit, we can find grace in the world and see how our work in community brings strength and joy.

Regarding despair, well, last week alone was probably enough to sink many of us. There was the video of Alton Sterling being killed by police in Baton Rouge. Then there was Philando Castile killed by police in a suburb of Minneapolis. Five Dallas police officers were killed while protecting peaceful protestors. That's only naming some of the violence in the streets of the United States.

In the midst of all that, you might have missed President Obama's announcement that he would keep 8,500 troops in Afghanistan indefinitely, perpetuating what is and has become an endless war. That endless war is also fueled by the so-called security assistance that our country provides through financial and military aid to countries around the world, as well as the low-intensity drone warfare we perpetuate.

The White House's statement on drones a couple weeks ago indicated that there had been 68 civilians killed by lethal drones in the last eight years. That number is far below the civilian count of deaths that many close observers of lethal drone warfare, and even journalists, have counted. Still, we count this action by the administration as a small step toward beginning to address transparency and accountability.

The drone program has often been off-limits to public debate because it is operated by the CIA. This report is an example of an opening where FCNL can step forward and request a meeting with security officials at the White House to talk about the drone program, and make it known that we oppose the use of lethal drones.

Today, Yasmine, who leads our civil rights and civil liberties and human rights program, is at the White House with other faith leaders—people from the Mennonite Church and the Church of the Brethren—to talk to members of the administration about the drone program and discuss our difficulty with how they term "civilians" and "non-combatants." They're also there to think about how to restrict this drone program.

Many of us turn off the news because we cannot bear to hear the repetitive speeches or, sometimes, the downright lies of candidates running for public office. At the same time, we may find it hard to look away from the historical shifts that we know our country and our world are going through. We are in a rapidly changing global society, and just keeping up can consume us. If we look at injustice from a strictly political perspective, we do have reasons to be discouraged. Congress, as you know, is more partisan than ever. I was at a conference about three weeks ago put on by a security think tank where Vice President Joe Biden spoke.

He said, specifically, that in the last four years he has seen Congress become more partisan than ever. Seeking policy changes to promote peaceful solutions to deadly conflict, address human security threats, address systemic injustices, meaningfully reduce carbon emissions, or reform our broken immigration system can feel impossible if our elected officials won't take up the issues.

I will tell you that from my view of lobbying the front lines of Congress—and I literally have a view of the Hart Office Building, where many senators have their offices, because that's where our office is located—I can assure you that Friends are having an impact. We are having significant impact because of our network of Friends who have engaged.

Right now, there's a bill moving through Congress called The Genocide and Atrocities Prevention Act. It is a piece of legislation that creates an architecture for peacebuilding within the U.S. government. This legislation is the legacy of work that FCNL has done for well over a decade. A former Friend in residence here, Brigit Noyce, a former employee at FCNL, helped start the Peaceful Prevention of Deadly Conflict program at FCNL.

We now have a secretary for a peacebuilding policy, and we convene a coalition of about 26 human rights, humanitarian, religious, and development organizations. These organizations often have people on the front lines of deadly conflict working to try to implement peacebuilding solutions. Our work is trying to help create structures to support their work within the U.S. government.

We are trying to create structures so that when deadly conflict is brewing the first response is not to send in the U.S. military, but to prevent the conflict from escalating— to prevent war, in essence. If it weren't for FCNL, this legislation would not exist. Our staff worked with the staff of Sen. Ben Cardin (MD), who introduced the legislation.

Moreover, it was the FCNL advocacy network that resulted in us now having 12 Democrats and three Republican senators co-sponsoring this legislation. After the three Republicans signed, they called the Quakers and others who had lobbied them to say, "I signed on as a co-sponsor to this legislation."

So, they're paying attention. Later this month, for those of us who cannot look away from politics, we'll be watching the Republican and Democratic conventions on television. These are national events designed to be partisan, and they are also obviously designed to nominate the various parties' candidates. Of course, this is a historic year in many regards.

We now have the first woman to be nominated in a major party, and even if you don't like her, that is a "whoop whoop," OK? It's a good thing. We now have our first non-politician reality TV personality to be nominated by a major party. So again, from the political perspective, this is fascinating.

But when we move out of that political framework and consider what is happening in the world today from our spiritual condition and from a humanitarian and communitarian viewpoint, the view changes. We can see that we are not alone. There are millions of people around this country and around the world who long for an end to violence—not just Quakers, Mennonites, and Brethren. There are millions of people who are motivated to live nonviolently and peacefully, and who would like our elected officials to work on that.

There are thousands of organizations working to address climate change and lessen environmental degradation. There are 190 governments that have signed on to address and reduce carbon emissions, which they declared at the Paris climate conference. I know that that is not enough, but we are part of a broader community working to make the world a better place.

There are academics in our colleges and universities who are teaching students about conflict prevention and transitional justice and how to end and prevent wars so new ones don't start. There are also thousands of activists on the ground—many of them Quaker colleagues in Kenya, Burundi, Rwanda—working to prevent violent conflict. These are peacebuilding practitioners.

I often think of our peacebuilding work as having this academic, *in-the-ivory-tower* possibility, as well as people on the ground who are making it happen. In-between are the policy makers who just don't get it yet. They must learn how to implement what's happening.

We are not alone. When we take into our hearts the troubles of this world, we may still feel discouragement. But we may also begin to hear the still, small voice that can give us clarity and drive to use our own voices in the public sphere—not to add to the cacophony, but to speak from the truth we know.

"Do not let your hearts be troubled." That's the first verse of the 14th chapter of John, in which Thomas and Philip, disciples of Jesus, are worried. This is the time of Passover, when Jesus is about to be crucified, and they don't know what's going on. They say, "We don't know where you are going. How can we know the way? Just show us the Father. That will be enough for us."

This is at the point in the story when Jesus promises the Holy Spirit to be with the disciples. So when I was preparing my remarks for today and looking at different translations—which is just amazing because there are 50 translations—I came across the New International Version translation, which I love. This is the verse:

> *"But the advocate" (The advocate, that's sometimes what we call lobbyists.), "the advocate, the Holy Spirit, whom the Father will send in my name, will teach you all things. And will remind you of everything I have said to you. Peace I leave with you, my peace I give you. I do not give you as the world gives. Do not let your hearts be troubled, and do not be afraid."*

Let's talk about fear for just a little bit. Fear is a true emotion that we all feel at one time or another, and sometimes that fear can lead to despair. Surely we have all felt the pounding of our hearts before we must do something scary. When I was a small child, I was terrified to go into my basement alone because I had two older brothers who figured out that they could go downstairs and jump out and scare me, and I would scream, which delighted them.

Later, when I was in my twenties, I was accosted in my driveway in daylight. I was not physically harmed, but emotionally scarred. I feared leaving my house for months, especially at night. It was when I was pregnant with my first child, and it was a fearful time for me.

We all have fears about physical harm that could happen to us. These fears cause us to do all kinds of things to protect ourselves and our property. This may include buying expensive security systems or fortifying ourselves with weapons. This response of fear is played out at both the personal level and the national level.

As a country, we have built our national security's confidence on militarization. The American public buys this militarization argument because those selling it play on our fears. That argument, about the fear of others, has spread militarization to our communities. Local police don riot gear to counter peaceful protesters or use armored personnel carriers to show force.

This show of force at the personal, local, and national levels may make people feel protected, but when we examine it through the crucible of our inner lives, through our lives in the Spirit, we realize that this outward show of strength has its limits.

This strength is limited because it is based on fear, not on love. Our lives in the Spirit teach us to love. When we put on the Spirit of love, we see our work through a different lens. Sometimes I like to think in images, and when I think about looking through a different lens, I think of going to the eye doctor.

When the doctor puts that machine up to you and starts testing what you can see more clearly, they'll ask, "Better like this, or like this? Like this, or like this?" as they shift the lenses back and forth. You get about three seconds to decide which is the best view, which can sometimes make you stumble or feel uncertain.

Sometimes our view of our public lives and our political activity is like rapid-changing lenses. We aren't sure of the clarity, of how the grounding of our spiritual lives creates the crispest view. But I maintain there is a direct link between our spiritual lives and our political lives—a link that is, perhaps, even clearer for Quakers, because of the practice of our faith, than for many others.

Fear is, of course, not always physical. I know we also have fears of inadequacy. Will I be hired for that job? If I get the job, will I be successful? Will I have enough money to live through my retirement? Will I be loved? Those fears can extend to our spiritual and political practice as well. Are we Quakerly enough? If Diane expects me to talk to elected officials, will I know what to say? Will I have the confidence to ask a good question or make a good statement?

Well, I have some advice I'd like to share today about our spiritual and political lives—ideally, to help ease some of these fears and offer encouragement.

First, as the Religious Society of Friends, we have a powerful voice for peace and justice. We can and should speak boldly when we have something to say that has not been said or has not been heard. Second, we—as individuals, citizens, and people who care about the public welfare and life in this country and around the globe—must engage in the political system. Good citizenship requires more than voting. Finally, it is possible through our actions to have an impact on bending the arc of history toward justice.

Thinking about the role of the Religious Society of Friends—including participants in our meetings, members, attendees, admirers, companions along the way, and those who aspire to be connected to Quakers—we play a special role in this work.

Those who have been in this faith and practice of Friends for a long time are elders in a sense, holding meetings in the Light, serving on committees, contributing time and money, praying for the work of Quaker organizations around the globe, and going the extra mile. It's also about praying for the network of people around the country who are engaged with their elected officials.

I grew up in a Lutheran church, a church that had a U.S. flag and a Lutheran flag. The pastor would, at the end of every worship service, pray for the leaders of our country. I never understood it until I arrived in Washington, D.C.

That's when I started praying more than I had ever prayed. I gained a new understanding of Paul's encouragement to "[p]ray without ceasing." But if you don't pray, I will ask you to do what Pope Francis encouraged people to do when he visited Washington, D.C., and "send us your good intentions."

We are not alone. We carry the legacy of generations before us. I'm not a historian, but you know the history of Friends—our Quaker *brand*. But it isn't just a brand; we are deep and wide. Those Friends among us who are working on addressing injustice of all kinds, who have worked for years on voting rights and civil rights, are going to have to keep working because those rights are deteriorating in some places.

Those who worked on LGBTQ rights are going to have to keep working on it because a lot of people still oppose that. We have work to do on immigration reform, ending mass incarceration. We have work to do preventing war and promoting peace. We even have work to do on understanding our own role in power and privileged dynamics.

I am encouraged because this is what Friends do. We let our lives speak. We don't do a lot of preaching or proselytizing— though we could stand to do this a little more because we need more Quakers! It wasn't until I began working at FCNL that I really began to appreciate FCNL's process of going to Quaker meetings and churches every two years and asking for input on our priorities.

I did it in Hartford Meeting before I came to FCNL, and thought, "Well, what do they do with that? What difference does it make what I say?" I've since learned that it makes a huge difference to know and understand what Friends tell us, because it is Friends (with the help of our policy committee) who decide what FCNL will work on. This grounding is incredibly powerful to me in my role.

We are a multi-issue organization. The beauty of being a multi-issue organization and the work we try to do as staff is in drawing connections between various issues. For example, we get to help people understand how climate change can drive conflict, which can drive migration, which can drive Islamophobia.

Once our priorities are named at our annual meeting, staff develops what we call "change strategies," to figure out what we can do. There's no question that our legislative priorities are very aspirational, but we try to be strategic and thoughtful and speak in a parlance that people can understand. Most importantly, we try to represent what Friends ask us to do, and we usually find a great way to do both.

FCNL was the first faith-based lobby—established in Washington, D.C., in 1943. As we approach 75, we are not as old as Fellowship of Reconciliation, but we are getting up there. We are also the largest faith-based lobby in D.C., which many people find hard to believe.

We have staff of 43 right now, including lobbyists who are on the Hill. Our staff also includes those who travel around the country, fundraisers, and business office staff. We also have our young fellows, who come spend a year with us after graduating college. Then, there are the two buildings we own, so our staff also includes someone who manages those buildings.

Then there are the tens of thousands of people around the country—Quakers and others who care about these issues and want to work with us for change. We are hoping to continue to expand these numbers. I invite everyone to attend FCNL's annual meetings and lobby with us. Members of Congress listen to their constituents. It is incredibly important.

An engaged citizenry can bring integrity to politics. Strength comes from this network, and it is essential for lawmakers to hear the voices of their constituents. Even when you think you know what they believe or that they already agree with you, they need to hear from you. Especially if they disagree with you, they need to hear from you. Even if you keep getting the same form letter in response, they need to hear from you. It takes more than voting.

Political activism is more than talking to the people who agree with you. It is finding people with whom you are in conflict and figuring out how to have a respectful conversation that finds some common ground, but also tries to take another step.

That's part of what we do when we lobby, and it's why lobbying is a spiritual exercise. I once told a friend of mine in Hartford who was experiencing some conflict with someone else in the Meeting and wanted to avoid that person, "Well, that's the work. We have to figure out how to deal with people we're in conflict with."

I know it can be much more enjoyable to sit around and maybe watch your favorite TV show, hike on Mt. Rainier, or do any number of things. But figuring out how to put in a little bit of time to engage with your member of Congress is important. Dare I say it might even bring you a sense of strength and joy to do it. FCNL can help you because our work also includes training people.

We have established 27 advocacy teams around the country—from Great Falls, Montana, to Olympia and

From Despair to Strength and Joy

Bellingham, Washington. These are people who have agreed to put a little more time into their advocacy work by building a community around FCNL's priority areas. They meet once a month and write letters, a way to build skills and build support. Though I believe we need one in every state, you don't have to be an advocacy team member to take action. We make it easy to act through our website. You can also just pick up the phone and call your members of Congress.

You can start with a simple "thank you." Earlier this week, I told José Woss, our lobbyist leading criminal justice and sentencing reform, I was coming to Pacific Yearly Meeting and asked what I should speak about here. He said, "Ask anyone from Montana to call Sen. Danes to say, 'Thank you.'" Here is a quick demonstration:

First, you pick up the phone and call the district office or the Washington office.

Then, you can say, "Hi, I am Diane. I'm calling to thank you for supporting the sentencing reform infractions act. I'm really concerned with fairness, with federal sentencing and with Congress taking the lead in reducing the incarceration rate in our country. I also want to tell you how pleased I am that Sen. Danes is working on a bipartisan basis. As a voter and a Quaker, I really value bipartisanship and hope the senator will provide leadership for bipartisan solutions to climate change as well."

In less than one minute, you've thanked and introduced the next priority of importance to you.

After I heard from José, I spoke with Amelia Kegan, our director for Domestic Policy, who said, "If the Democrats gain control of the senate in November, which is widely expected, Sen. Widen of Oregon is going to be the chair of the budget committee, which is the powerful tax-writing committee." She added, "Talk to Sen. Widen about the Earned Income Tax Credit for single adults."

So here, when I call, I would say, "Sen. Widen, I'm calling to ask you to support making the Earned Income Tax Credit for single adults more effective. As a leader on the finance committee, your support of this would mean that millions of single adults who are working in low-wage jobs and not raising children could be lifted out of poverty, just as the Earned Income Tax Credit for Families helps families get out of poverty. Thank you so much."

That's it. It takes about a minute, but there are many issues where members of Congress do not know what their constituents think. They do not know what you believe. There are some things that they get dozens of calls on, and there are many things they get very few calls on. You can have an influence.

You should also know that persistence makes a difference. It is great to send an email and make a phone call, but following up a month or two later is even better. We talk about building engagement, building a relationship with Congress. Do you want to know how to do that? It takes consistency. There are Friends here who have, over years, talked to their members of Congress about militarization or other key issues so much that the members start remembering them. They say, "Oh yeah, you're here to talk to me about that weapons system, right? Let's talk about it," and they pay attention. Jim Corbett, a leader in the Sanctuary movement in the 1980s famously said, "Individuals can resist injustice, but only in community can we do justice."

The mutual support of our meetings and of those who go with us is very important. Justice in community brings me to my third and final point, a phrase you know well from Dr. Martin Luther King Jr.: "The arc of the moral universe is long, but it bends towards justice." Our collective action is what helps to bend the arc of the moral universe.

The inherent detail, which you can appreciate more and more as you get older, is that we won't always see the fruits of our labor. We won't always see a lovely arc. As with voting rights or LGBTQ rights, it may bend toward justice, and then it may get a little crooked again and kind of bounce back up. Another example of this is the Iran deal. A year ago today, President Obama announced that the U.N. Security Council had come to an agreement with Iran about its nuclear program, forbidding the country from acquiring a nuclear weapon.

This is an issue that FCNL has worked on for a long time, to try to create diplomacy with Iran. We employed a full-scale lobbying effort when that announcement came out. We worked with religious communities around Washington. We held a national call with the National Council of Churches and Pax Christi International. We mobilized people, particularly in Maryland, Pennsylvania, Connecticut, New York, and North Dakota, to try to get the 41 senators who would support this. We were successful. It was a remarkable achievement.

Iran has dismantled its nuclear program and cannot now acquire a nuclear weapon, which will continue. This is an important step in nuclear non-proliferation and disarmament. Unfortunately, however, the arc may not stay in place. This week the House introduced a bill to impose new sanctions. Iran is not an easy partner to work with. They continue to violate human rights. The work is not done.

We know that to move from despair to strength and joy, we must walk into conflict to do the work of justice. We must talk and listen to people who disagree with us to find strength. We must relish the act of faithfulness in the spirit of love to experience joy.

I would like to close with a quote from Reinhold Niebuhr, a well-known Christian realist theologian from the 1940s and 1950s, who wrote a book called, *The Irony of American History*:

> *"Nothing that is worth doing can be achieved in our lifetime. Therefore we must be saved by hope. Nothing which is true or beautiful or good makes complete sense in the immediate context of history. Therefore we must be saved by faith. Nothing we do, however virtuous, can be accomplished alone. Therefore we must be saved by love. No virtuous act is quite as virtuous from the standpoint of our friend or foe as it is from our own standpoint. Therefore we must be saved by the final form of love, which is forgiveness."*

From Despair to Strength and Joy

We are not alone. We know the Spirit is in us and with us. We know that the undivided life, when we let our inward experience inform our outward action to live in the world, can help us let go of despair. We can move with strength and hope and with joy. Our participation in community brings us hope; our life in the Spirit brings us joy and brings us peace. Not as the world gives. Let not your hearts be troubled, neither let them be afraid.

A sign campaign from FCNL made many appearances during Pacific Yearly Meeting 2016.

Photo by Jennifer Domenick/FCNL

Spirit-Led Social Action

Carey Memorial Lecture » Baltimore Yearly Meeting
Oct. 13, 2016 » Frostburg, MD

I believe that a Spirit-led life leaves us no choice but social action. In Luke 10, we are told that Jesus was asked by a religious scholar for the path to inheriting eternal life. Jesus posed the question back to him, "What does the law say?" to which the scholar answered, "You shall love the Lord your God with all your heart with all your soul and with all your strength and all your mind. And love your neighbor as yourself."

These commandments to love God completely and to love our neighbor appear in other chapters of the Bible as well—both the Old and New Testaments. But what do these verses teach us about being Spirit-led and leading lives of social action today?

Above: Diane with Senator Chuck Grassley (IA) and FCNL's Jim Cason.

First, they teach us to love God entirely and to not hold back. How to love God with our heart, soul, and mind—or as The Message translation of the Bible says, with our passion, prayer, intelligence, and energy—is not always obvious.

In my experience, loving God is as much about relaxing into God's love as it is about any specific action I might take. I cannot earn my way into God's love. I am in God's love; we all are. In 1661, Isaac Pennington wrote these words to encourage a surrender to the divine love that centers us:

> *"Give over thine own willing, give over thine own running, give over thine desiring to know or to be anything and sink down to the Seed which God sows in thy Heart and let that be in thee and grow in thee and breathe in thee and act in thee and thou shall find by sweet experience that the Lord knows that and loves that, and will lead it to the inheritance of life, which is his portion."*

What does "You shall love your neighbor as yourself" teach us about social action? Simply, it instructs us to love our neighbor.

I take a broad definition of neighbor. It can mean the person sitting next to you tonight, the people you live next door to whose dog barks annoyingly at every sound, the people in your meeting who always arrive late for worship, or the Quakers around the world whose theology is different than your own. To me, it means the Christians, Jews, Muslims, and non-believers whose attitudes and beliefs are different than yours; it means the people in your community with whom you disagree politically; it means the poor and the wealthy.

To illustrate what he meant by loving your neighbor, Jesus told the parable of the Good Samaritan. Modern-day Quakers are not always as familiar with the Bible as our predecessors. In my own meeting, I have seen struggles in First Day School over how to teach the Bible. However, our children learned the story of the Good Samaritan thoroughly. Perhaps more than any other, this Bible story tells us the Christian expectation of mercy and social action.

A man who is traveling on the road from Jerusalem is beaten, robbed, and left to die. In an unexpected twist for those hearing this story when Jesus told it, the Samaritan, who would have been the last person expected to stop and help, is the person who shows mercy to the stranger who was robbed and beaten. And Jesus said, "Go and do likewise."

This radical notion that Jesus taught of responding with love to a stranger, even to an enemy, was as counter-intuitive in biblical times as it is today. We often have difficulty practicing it, but we recognize it in others. I have witnessed this quality of mercy in areas where conflict is evident, and violence is not far.

When I traveled to the Middle East last year with Jonathan Evans, FCNL's then-foreign policy representative, we visited Jim and Debbie Fine, Friends from Philadelphia Yearly Meeting, and Ann Ward of this yearly meeting who were working for the Mennonite Central Committee in Erbil, Iraq. We drove to Sulaymaniyah, a city in the Kurdish region of Iraq, to meet with local leaders.

Fresh with the fever of the nonviolent movements sweeping through North Africa that spring, they had organized peaceful demonstrations calling for greater transparency and accountability from political leaders in Iraq. At the home of the Christian Peacemakers, we heard from organizers of their passionate calls for justice for the deaths of 10 people who had been killed in peaceful demonstrations. Committed to nonviolence, these organizers had found solidarity with the Christian Peacemakers, whose presence exemplified the essence of loving your neighbor.

In Palestine, we visited Bethlehem, where—adjacent to the separation wall that looks and feels like a penitentiary wall shadowing the Wi'Am: The Palestinian Conflict Transformation Center—we were only a couple of kilometers from the site of Jesus' birthplace. We traveled to Hebron and walked the market, talking to a vendor whose stall sat beneath the fencing that separated the Palestinian area from a Jewish school built in the settlement, from which the school children sometimes threw rocks.

We visited Sister Paulette Schroeder and other young adults who were part of the Christian Peacemaker team in the Hebron region, providing accompaniment to Palestinian young men who were often harassed and faced intimidation and violence. In their home, they had a photo of Tom Fox, who gave his life as a witness for peace.

This past spring, I had the opportunity to see the ways that Quakers and other people of faith in Kenya are practicing peacemaking in areas that saw violent conflict following the last national elections at the end of 2007 and into 2008. Getry Azigah of Friends Church Peace Teams is providing leadership among Kenyan Friends and working closely with David Zarembka of the African

Great Lakes Initiative, whose influence with Alternatives to Violence and other peacemaking initiatives in Kenya, Rwanda, and Burundi are practical applications of loving your neighbor in places where violent conflict and war have scarred lives and communities.

Getry Azigah (second from left) visited FCNL in May 2015. From left, she is joined by FCNL staffers Allyson Neville, Diane, Theo Sitther, and Sean Langberg.

Friends, we are part of a faith community with nearly 400 years of Spirit-led social action. Friends who have worked to end slavery, establish civil rights, lift people from poverty, promote peace and reconciliation are our historic calling cards.

To what is the Spirit leading us today? What social action is your measure?

As John Woolman's words encourage us, "To turn all we possess into the channel of universal love becomes the business of our lives." When we can be and act in that spirit of love, others see it. We are witnessing then to the power of love. Many of our brothers and sisters live this kind of

Spirit-led life that makes love the first motion of all social action. All of us aspire to it.

This is the essence of social action—loving our neighbors as ourselves. It manifests in countless ways; it can be witness for equality, truth, justice, and peace. It can be a protector of our planet. It can be builder of community or caregiver of the vulnerable. It is always grounded in Spirit.

A few months ago, I spent a weekend at a retreat with heads of other Quaker organizations who do service and advocacy at a national or international level. As we began to summarize our conversations, the facilitator used the term *moral authority* to describe our *Quaker voice* in peacemaking and how others regard us.

I liked that term because, as one who is an avid consumer of political news, I believe we have a deep hunger for morality in public life. The small group of Friends gathered was not in agreement on that term; others suggested *authentic voice*, rather than *moral voice*, to describe a Quaker stance for peace and justice.

This probably more accurately reflects the idea that our center, the Spirit that gives rise to our social action, requires us to be authentic. It requires us to live with integrity, to be single in our lives—from the way we live—to the actions we take. This authentic voice is a natural expression of our inward condition.

Giving voice to the possibilities for healing the earth, for building a community where every person's potential may be fulfilled, for social justice and equity, and for a world free of war are the natural expressions of a Spirit-filled life.

You may be wondering what any of this has to do with FCNL and lobbying. Well, can you guess who our neighbor is?

Directly across the street from FCNL, our neighbor is the Hart Senate office building that is home to 50 U.S. senators. About two blocks away are the U.S. Capitol and the Supreme Court. Sen. Mitch McConnell (KY) lives right down the street, and Sen. Barbara Boxer (CA) lives around the corner.

So when I talk about being Spirit-led to social action, and I talk about social action based on Jesus' admonition to love our neighbors, I am also talking about the U.S. Congress. This is really a test for most of us to understand that the encouragement to love our neighbors means loving the people who have the power to change systems but who can't even mention the words "climate change," who hold the purse strings to prioritize spending for human needs over militarization, who are held up as leaders but often devolve into partisan bickering.

As clearly as I have heard any message from the Spirit, I hear this: Love your neighbor as yourself—especially those in political power.

For nearly 75 years, FNCL has worked as a Quaker lobby, advancing a vision of loving our neighbors. Many of you in Baltimore Yearly Meeting have been led to use your authentic voices in unity with FCNL—to advocate for ending conscription, for civil rights, for immigration reform, for sustainable energy sources, for preventing war and promoting peace and disarmament.

Spirit-Led Social Action

You have extended the practice of loving your neighbor by promoting peace and justice for our neighbors in this country and around the world.

I want to say this to you: Don't stop. Renew your strength. Now as much as any other time, your elected officials need to hear your authentic voice. They need to hear the authentic voice that arises from your spiritual grounding, and they need to hear what you know from your experience.

They need to hear from those of you who work in prisons, teach children, or build housing for people who are disabled or poor. They need to hear from those of you who run businesses, who care for the elderly, who are students, and who are retired. They need to hear from school administrators, insurance agents, mechanics, factory workers, and medical technicians. They need to hear from the unemployed. You are in the family of Friends who have historically and steadfastly stood for peace and for justice.

You see directly what misplaced priorities of spending our national treasure—over $600 billion this year—on the military means when local communities are forced to reduce food stamps, fire teachers, or defer infrastructure investments. You see the devastation that befalls families whose loved ones are killed, maimed, are scarred forever by the human costs of war. You recognize the moral harm that comes from relying only on the powers of military might when we know that prevention of war is more cost-effective.

What difference does your voice make? Why should you bother to take the social action of being a grassroots lobbyist for the issues you care about?

As I travel among Friends, I'm often asked about the gridlock in Washington and whether it really matters to write a letter or send an email. Let's face it: Quakers share the same frustrations as our fellow citizens do with elected officials in their bickering and seeming inability to solve the thorny domestic and foreign policy problems of the United States.

The approval rating of Congress is less than 10%. But we as Friends just might have a greater belief than many of our fellow citizens in *the common good*—the notion that our government can and does serve the people.

And when we are Spirit-led in our social action, we have an authentic voice. It is a voice that those representatives we have elected to work for us in Washington need to hear.

If you don't use your voice for a world free of war, for an earth restored, who will? How do you want your representatives and senators to set priorities in the federal budget? Should we reduce the federal deficit through cuts to domestic spending and changing entitlements but not touch the Pentagon's budget? Should Congress appropriate more funding to the State Department for programs that peacefully prevent deadly conflict?

Do you think continuing to have military troops in Afghanistan is a good idea? Would you favor reductions in nuclear weapons? Do you think there is a compelling moral reason for Congress to address climate change? Should the United States exercise all diplomatic means to prevent war with Iran? Should we ensure that Native American women have protection against domestic violence?

Spirit-Led Social Action

FCNL represents all these issues and more. I cannot say enough about the deep reservoir of support, encouragement, and prayers that Friends throughout the country give to FCNL's work. However, not one of the 100 senators or 435 representatives work for FCNL, the organization. They work for the people who can vote for them. To be sure, they listen to FCNL's voice; our staff have good working relationships with offices on the Hill that contribute to our effectiveness. But members of Congress need to hear from those they represent.

The more compelling reason why we speak to those in political power is the Spirit leading or perhaps even pushing us to extend ourselves, to take risks. It is through spiritual grounding that we are called to speak and act.

If you have ever experienced the call to give vocal ministry in silent worship, you may relate to the feeling of hesitation, of not wanting to rise and speak, but recognizing that you are compelled to stand and deliver a message—however inarticulate you may feel. You don't have the responsibility for how others in the worship hear your message; you have responsibility to be authentic to the Spirit in delivering the message.

While I know that lobbying a member of Congress and speaking in worship are two quite distinct actions, the motion of love may well be the same.

As you can tell, I believe lobbying is crucial to our Spirit-led social action. It is a well-established tradition within the Religious Society of Friends. From George Fox to Margaret Fell to Elizabeth Fry, Quakers have used our voices to press

147

those who have political power to change systems that—as Dr. Martin Luther King Jr. said—bend the long arc of history toward justice.

I invite you to consider whether the Spirit is leading you to build a relationship with your elected official, to love the neighbor who is your senator or representative in Congress. I invite you to test this on November 15 and 16 at the Quaker Public Policy Institute that FCNL is organizing as an opportunity for Friends and others to learn and lobby on the significant federal budget decisions that face us right now.

Learning to let the Spirit, and not my political passions, lead is a spiritual practice for me. I get angry; I am disappointed; I can be cynical about politics and power. But I can't ignore the power of the Spirit that teaches love. I return to prayer, spiritual reading, and corporate worship to sink down to the Seed, and to love God with muscle and passion. I ask for support from others and try to hold myself lightly. Without this grounding, advocating for peace and justice loses its joy and its power.

I will conclude with the words of Rufus Jones; I didn't find the Carey Lecture he delivered in 1947, but had he been speaking on Spirit-led social action, these might have been in his remarks:

> *"The first state of 'entry into life' for Jesus is learning to love. To start executing a 'social program' without the creative and motive power of a great love behind it is like building a factory and forgetting to attach the machinery to any driving energy that would turn the wheels."*

Friends, the Spirit is present and ready to lead and sustain us. May our social action be attached to the driving energy of the Spirit's love. May we love God with all our hearts, our souls, our strength, and our minds. And may we love our neighbors as ourselves.

Healing the Heart of Democracy

FCNL 2016 Annual Meeting » November 11, 2016 » Washington, DC

How do we respond to the political offenses that tear at the dignity of human beings? Do we respond based on their religion, their ethnic background, their gender, or their appearance? How do we respond to our neighbors, relatives, or coworkers who want to "drain the swamp" that they perceive is Washington, D.C.? Several passages are helping me answer these questions:

II Timothy 1:7 reads, "For God has not given us a spirit of fear but of power and love and of a sound mind."

Similarly, "Advices," from New England Yearly Meeting Faith and Practice, reads,

> *"The power of God is not used to compel us to Truth; therefore, let us renounce for ourselves the power of any person over any other and, compelling no one; let us seek to lead others to Truth through love. Let us teach by being ourselves teachable. Friends are advised to witness to the power of Truth and justice and to foster growth of the divine community at home and abroad.*
>
> *While remaining faithful to our Quaker insights, and ready to share them with others, let us seek to understand the contributions made by the people of God everywhere. Whenever possible, let us seek to enter into prayer and work with the wider community of faith."*

Parker J. Palmer wrote, "Political civility is not about being polite to each other. It's about reclaiming the power of 'We the People' to come together, debate the common good, and call American democracy back to its highest values amid our differences."

Finally, George Fox said, "I saw also that there was an ocean of darkness and death, and an infinite ocean of light and love, which flowed over the ocean of darkness."

On Wednesday, when staff gathered to begin processing the surprising results of the election, I asked them to look inward—to reflect on what is the source of their own power. What in our souls moves us to act for peace, stand up against injustice, or strive to reverse the causes of climate change? What calls us to #lovethyneighbor without exceptions and lets love be the first motion?

As I have tried to clear my mind in preparation for our time together in worship today, I couldn't move from the leading that in our gathering and in this time of worship, we need to confront the darkness—not just of the election season, but the darkness of humanity.

During this year,

» we've witnessed in our handheld devices the deadly violence against Black men and women at the hands of police;

» we've seen evil done by people whose rage spurs murder because of the race or sexual preference or profession of others—in Orlando, San Bernardino, Dallas, Kalamazoo, Washington, Louisiana;

» we've seen the violence of war and deadly conflict in Syria, Yemen, Burundi, Nigeria, and elsewhere;

» we've seen terrorist attacks—in the Middle East, in the United States, in Pakistan, in Europe, and in other parts of the globe;

» we've seen the violation of human rights and blatant disregard for international law by nation states;

» we've seen the rise of dictatorial and nationalist leaders who have the popular support of their people;

» we've witnessed our planet warming, our seas rising, Indigenous people displaced from their livelihoods and sacred ground;

>> we've heard Muslims, Mexicans, women, and people with disabilities vilified;

>> we've seen the harsh reality of anger and fear in the American electorate by many people;

>> we see immigrants and refugees whose lives are torn apart and who are at great risk of harm and detention; and

>> we see the people on the streets of almost every city and town and in every rural county who are homeless, hungry, hurting, and often hopeless.

As Quakers, we don't have liturgy in our worship for the confession of sins. In fact, Quakers don't talk about sin much at all, but we do acknowledge the darkness within us and within society, just as we acknowledge the Light within.

Within every one of us there is the power of darkness but also the infinite power of light and love. So let us together, with humility, confront this darkness that exists in the world—in us and other human beings. And together, let us take on the spirit of power and love and use the sound minds that God has given us.

How do we do this? How do we confront darkness and take on the spirit of power and love? I want to talk about two ways we do that within the FCNL community—that is, those of you gathered today and the wider community of people who act with FCNL.

First, using the sound minds God gave us, we look at root causes of problems and try to find the solutions. And as much as possible, we look for solutions that have bipartisan support. That means we may move more slowly than we want. It means we must compromise on the immediate step—that is the nature of political engagement—but we do not compromise our vision or our understanding of the root causes of problems.

This body has created a policy statement that guides us. I encourage you to re-read FCNL's powerful policy statement; you will be refreshed in what we have done together to name responses to darkness that feeds violence, war, degradation of our planet and harm to others.

Last year, when we gathered and we lobbied on peacebuilding, we were lobbying for the pragmatic steps toward a world free of war and the threats of war. FCNL has worked for well over a decade to identify and offer solutions to complement our famous bumper sticker, "War Is Not the Answer." Peacebuilding, the peaceful prevention of deadly conflict, diplomacy, strengthening international institutions dedicated to arms control—these are solutions.

Our newly released report, "A Necessary Good: U.S. Leadership on Preventing Mass Atrocities," is another step forward in our lobby to end war and build peace. The bipartisan group of Washington, D.C., experts we convened to help with this report will be offering this to the Trump administration as a pragmatic and powerful set of recommendations for U.S. foreign policy.

As you lobbied yesterday for criminal justice sentencing reform and as our Advocacy Corps lobbies in their local districts for immigration reform, we are working for a society with equity and justice for all.

As we lobby for Native American issues, we are lobbying for a society with equity and justice and for communities in which all peoples' potential might be fulfilled. We are recognizing that the European-American-centric view cannot be the normative viewpoint for our public policies if we are about creating equality.

This brings me to the second way we can take on the spirit of power and love spoken of in II Timothy. It is that we cultivate habits of the heart. In his book, *Healing the Heart of Democracy*, Parker Palmer talks about five habits of the heart:

» To understand that we are all in this together.

» To develop an appreciation of the value of *otherness*.

» To cultivate the ability to hold tension in life-giving ways.

» To generate a sense of personal voice and agency.

» To strengthen our capacity to create community.

We understand that we're all in this together; that the problems of a warming planet affect us all; that the proliferation of nuclear weapons puts everyone at risk; that income inequality is a problem for everyone—poor, rich, and middle class—and for the very fabric of our society.

When we develop an appreciation of the value of *otherness*, we become a little less selfish. We begin to open our world view to how others see things.

Some of you saw me last January when I was on crutches following surgery for a broken ankle. I can tell you that the short experience I had in not being 100% mobile made me appreciate those whose mobility is impaired by health or age.

I don't have to personally worry about being attacked or persecuted because of my religion, but I appreciate that my Muslim sisters and brothers are way too often seen as *other* in our communities and that Islamophobia is alive and dangerous and may have just received an accelerant in this election.

When we cultivate the ability to hold tension in life-giving ways, we accept our own imperfections and the imperfections of those around us. We accept contradictions; I accept that I am a spiritual being operating in the very worldly setting of Washington, D.C. I accept that what separates me from a person who has the opposite political viewpoint is not insurmountable because we are both beloved children of God.

We have generated a sense of personal voice and agency. This is our work to use our personal agency to speak to our elected officials. Our Advocacy Corps and Advocacy Teams, your emails and phone calls, your visits on the Hill yesterday, and the in-district visits you will do in December—all of these generate personal voice and agency.

As for Parker Palmer's fifth habit of the heart, "to strengthen our capacity to create community," you are here; you have this community that welcomes and embraces you. We encourage each other; sometimes we challenge each other.

We see that of God in each other. We see the dignity, the worth, the value in one another. As we know the benefits of this community, I hope you'll encourage others to join us—to sign up for FCNL emails and take action, to help create an Advocacy Team, to get others in your meeting or church to come to lobby with us, to participate in this Spirit-led action.

Staying clear about the root causes of problems, acting now for pragmatic policy solutions, practicing the habits of the heart—these are ways that we confront darkness. These practices help me stay grounded in Spirit-led action.

What is the internal source of your power? What moves in you to cry out, to speak out, to act out?

For me, this power comes from the source I name Holy Spirit. It is the Spirit Jesus promised to us in John 14:27, "Peace I leave with you; My peace I give unto you, not as the world giveth, give I unto you. Let not your heart be troubled, neither let it be afraid."

This peace of the Holy Spirit comforts and compels me. It comforts me to let my heart not be troubled or afraid, even if my head is troubled. It compels me to act based on what I know in my soul—that God has not given us a spirit of fear but of power and love and sound mind. Let us use that Spirit for our action together.

Standing in the Light:
Power, Politics, and Prophecy

FCNL 2017 Annual Meeting » November 5, 2017 » Washington, DC

"Truth is one and the same always, though ages and generations pass away, and one generation goes, and another comes, yet the word and the power of the Living God endures forever, and is the same and never changes."

— *Margaret Fell (1614-1702)*

Tonight, my message is about power, politics, and prophecy. It is about the collective power we share and the individual power we live into. It is about how the fierce urgency of now calls us to the prophetic work of loving our neighbors with no exception.

What does it mean to stand in the Light? For me, it is knowing how to make meaning and be alive in the world.

My Quaker faith and practice, shaped by the belief that the Spirit lives in me and in each of us, that this Spirit gives life to my witness and practice—this inward movement compels my witness in the world. The essence of who we are at FCNL and how we witness in the world is grounded in the faith and practice of the Religious Society of Friends. This witness is more than resistance; it is about being present with a prophetic vision of justice, grounded in love.

Let us name and claim what that world would be if

» we lived in a world free of war and the threat of war;

» we lived in a society with equity and justice for all;

» we lived in communities where every person's potential was fulfilled;

» we lived on an earth restored.

When I spoke to this gathering in 2011, the year I began as executive secretary of FNCL, I encouraged us to be bold, strategic, and relentless—and we have been. For the past 74 years, this organization has been respected on Capitol Hill and by Friends and other supporters across the country.

Seven years ago, FCNL had weathered the recession of 2008 and had received instructions from the General Committee to do more with young adults. The General Committee also took on the risk or purchasing the property adjacent to our office building, not yet knowing we would create a Quaker Welcome Center but knowing the value of a growing presence on Capitol Hill. Indeed, we knew the time was ripe for a capital campaign.

By seizing these opportunities to be bold in our witness, to build FCNL's presence on Capitol Hill and around the country, here is what we have done:

» Our staff has almost doubled.

» We've established a young adult program that brings FCNL to 60 campuses across the country and offers practical lobbying experiences to over 500 young adults each year.

» We've launched a new program called the Advocacy Corps, which equips 20 young adults to organize in their local communities over a 10-month period developing relationships with their members of Congress. We've established a formal summer internship program, and we've strengthened our yearlong Young Fellows program.

» We are becoming a more diverse organization, in both our staff and our program work. We take a broad view of diversity; certainly ethnic and socioeconomic diversity, but also age, theological, and political diversity are important to us. Moreover, we are striving to garner the benefits of being a more diverse organization by being a more inclusive organization.

» We have built a network of 80 Advocacy Teams in 36 states—over 1,000 people who are committed together to build relationships with their members of Congress.

» We are opening our Quaker Welcome Center on Capitol Hill to encourage Friends and others to witness every week. We are inviting staff, volunteers, and anyone passing by our busy location to a midweek time of silent reflection.

» We have seen a year-over-year increase in the number of lobby visits—both by our staff lobbyists and by our network across the country in local offices, building relationships with members of Congress and their staff—for peacebuilding, diplomacy, human rights, healthcare, criminal justice reform, compassionate immigration reform, support to refugees, Native American issues, and addressing climate change.

We have been empowered by the culture of trust established by our General Committee. The work we do to engage people across the country and Congress is premised on a relationship of trust—that we share common ground and that we can listen and act on Truth.

This trust, built through integrity and established relationships over decades for FCNL, is in the living stream of Friends' faithful witness over many centuries. Trust builds community and this community gives us a standing for faithful and effective advocacy. This enabled us to accomplish the following:

» Build relationships across the partisan divide on climate change that recognizes the imperative to act.

» Shepherd the Elie Wiesel Genocide and Atrocities Prevention Act that establishes stronger peacebuilding programs in our federal government.

» Lobby last year for an important bill on criminal justice sentencing reform—getting to the cusp of seeing this bill move forward, only to see it set aside in the political tsunami of 2016 election; but to be persistent in our advocacy for that legislation, which is once again advancing.

» Press relentlessly against the billions and billions of dollars that the administration and Congress shovel to the Pentagon, and sharing our personal stories about why it is wrong to allow one federal agency, the Department of Defense, to spend with impunity, with no audit or accountability for waste, fraud, and abuse.

» Carry out this David v. Goliath lobby initiative by citizens who are empowered to act in opposition to the glut of lobbyists who spend well over $100 million a year to perpetuate and grow defense contractors' business at taxpayers' expense.

» Protect the expansion of health care through the Affordable Care Act—particularly for people whose incomes are low, people who are working, and people who have disabilities or who are elderly and rely on Medicaid.

» Stand for religious freedom for people to worship, work, live, and thrive in our communities—whether Christian, Muslim, Jewish, or Quaker.

» Welcome refugees and immigrants—recognizing that the unprecedented number of refugees is caused by people fleeing violent conflict and economic hardship, understanding that compassionate and comprehensive immigration policy creates a stronger economy and stronger communities.

I am proud of the work we have done together—during my time leading FCNL and over the 68 years before I arrived. I am proud of our staff and the deep commitment of our Committee. We work hard and we make change. We lead with hope.

I'm ever grateful to Friend Tom Ewell who told me before I began working at FCNL, "We're very glad you are here, Diane, and we think you are going to be a great executive secretary. But, you should know, this organization isn't about you or only about the staff here—as great as they are (and they are great!). It's about the people around the country who created and sustain FCNL through their actions. It's about our role among Friends."

I am encouraged every time I think of Tom's counsel because I know that the weight of our work rests not only on what staff do, but on all of us who long for the beloved community and who support this work through prayers, good intentions, financial support, and lobbying of people across the country.

So, I tell you this evening, that as happy as I am to have all of you with us here in Washington at the Quaker Public Policy Institute and Annual Meeting, and as proud as I am of the over 250 lobby visits you have done over the past two days and of the hundreds of lobby visits you will do in the coming months, the state of our society, the condition of our country, the plight of our planet demands that we do more.

We cannot be satisfied or rest easily about our successful capital campaign or our growth of Advocacy Teams. We cannot rest on our 75-year history or Quaker values, on our moral grounding, or on our successes.

We can and do stand on this powerful foundation. But, Friends, we are operating under governmental power structures—in this country and in countries around the world—that are a threat to humanity.

People across the globe are being killed in deadly conflict by weapons made in the United States. The U.S. military is fueling the Saudi airplanes that are wreaking the worst humanitarian crisis since World War II in Yemen. Civilians are being killed and starved.

What we have known as the existential threat of nuclear war is made more real by the taunting, bullying, and lies of Donald Trump and Kim Jung Un.

We are not only negating any movement toward the vision of Shared Security; our president has slammed the door on diplomacy—from decertifying the Iran deal to pulling out of the Paris climate accord, our country is walking away from the diligent and demanding labor of diplomacy.

As one of the biggest contributors to carbon output in the world, we are pulling back on the commitments we made to the other 190 nations that signed the Paris Climate Accord in 2015 and to families and neighborhoods that have counted on the protections of the Environmental Protection Agency.

At the same time, we have an administration that is radically retrenching through dramatic changes in the federal budget and federal agencies while pushing for a hugely regressive tax restructuring. Our government—of the people, by the people, and for the people—is being twisted to serve a narrow segment of our society. We may not see the results of these shifts immediately, but they will be felt for generations to come.

The structural racism built into our public policies over generations that subjugate people with brown or black skin to different standards—from criminal justice to public education to healthcare to housing opportunity—is now more overt with brazen demands and displays from white supremacists that are accepted by our president.

The grievous acts of white supremacy exhibited in Charlottesville presented a full affront to what many African Americans and other people of color have experienced throughout their lives—behavior that demeans, degrades, and rejects anyone other than *white*. The fault lines of whiteness that make true equality a lie are deep and touch every one of us.

Knowing this, where do we stand? How do we stand in the Light? Do we hear the still small voice or a roaring outrage or a finely honed love that leads us to act? Are we moving into proximity of oppression, conflict, and injustice? How does each of us show up in this mission for FCNL—"to live a prophetic Quaker vision for a peaceful, just, and healthy planet through education, lobbying, and grassroots advocacy?"

Perhaps, even more importantly, how do we "live into the virtue that takes away the occasion for war?" When we are touched by the Sacred or the Light or by God or by the Power that is greater than any one of us, we yearn for wholeness. We find violence intolerable; we are in pain for the earth; we suffer the injustice of people whose dignity is disregarded and disdained because of their religion, their race, their gender, or their sexual identity.

Using our power is not about the politics of partisanship or political parties. It is not about the power of money, of domination, or of empire. It is about the power of people, of human beings.

Two months ago, I traveled to the Middle East on a delegation with the National Council of Churches. We met with Muslim and Christian leaders and with government officials and activists. We visited the presidential palace in Egypt, replete with chandeliers and high security, and met with el-Sisi.

We visited the dusty, hot Hebron Hills in Palestine and met with Issa Amro, a human rights activist who uses the power of nonviolence to confront the occupation of Israeli settlers. The subject of human rights and religious freedom were discussed with everyone; the desire to be recognized and respected as human beings who can live in peace is universal.

The other universal message is the hope that we will recognize that every action our government takes has a corresponding reaction across the globe.

For FCNL, the evolution of our direction in the next five years began even before the political turmoil of this past year. It began through the commitment we made in "The World We Seek: Now Is the Time" capital campaign to grow our young adult programs and create a Quaker Welcome Center, to create an endowment for the Friend in Washington program and for our lobbying.

When the Forward Planning Working Group brought its recommendations to this gathering last year, it was the fruit of nine months of labor together in 2016 to outline organizational priorities and a mission statement. It was before the seismic shift of our politics was confirmed by the election of Donald Trump. It turns out that the priorities named by that Forward Planning working group were prescient for FCNL; you might even say prophetic. Our direction in the next five years has power.

Because of the powerful foundation of Friends, because of our Quaker practice of listening to the Spirit, because of the imagination and efforts of so many of you, I believe that in the next five years, we can take bold steps to transform national policy discourse and decision-making.

We can build political will for legislation and public policy change that reflects our legislative priorities. Our relentless advocacy on Capitol Hill and in congressional districts throughout the country will strengthen constituent voices and offer a compelling narrative for what we value: peace and social justice and empowering civil dialogue for policy change by Congress.

This will require a bigger presence for FCNL—in the media, on Capitol Hill, and in congressional districts across the country. It will require the vital support of Quakers and all people who share our vision and mission.

Our organizational structure and programs will adapt as we continue to become a more diverse and inclusive organization, increasing the representation and meaningful involvement of Quakers and people from many ethnic and socioeconomic backgrounds. We are more powerful through the diversity of our staff and dedicated volunteers. We will nurture an FCNL culture that recognizes that of God in every person, affirms individual strengths, and cultivates organizational excellence.

Advancing effective public policies through federal legislation is the heart of FCNL's mission. Fielding a Capitol Hill lobbying team that brings subject matter expertise and strategic political analytics to our work is essential to our faithful representation of FCNL's legislative priorities for peace, justice, and sustainability. Relationships with congressional offices and with coalition partners matter to the effectiveness of our Capitol Hill work.

We've seen the power of constituent advocacy as the way to influence Congress.

Last week, I attended a Ploughshares Fund conference where several members of Congress spoke. Rep. Adam Smith of Seattle, who does have a relationship with FCNL, said this to my question about what we should be doing to motivate Congress to prevent a confrontation with North Korea or to preserve the Iran Deal: "The best thing you can do is get into the offices of the 535 members of Congress on a consistent basis. Let them know you are watching and expecting action."

FCNL's strategic advocacy network enables us to do just that. In fact, an effective grassroots advocacy program coupled with our registered lobbyists make FCNL a powerful operation. Constituent voices matter to members of Congress. Influencing the policy conversation from the local level has huge importance. Persistent constituents speak to the needs of their communities, and they can open doors for our lobbyists on Capitol Hill. FCNL's network provides a way for people around the country to have a meaningful impact on national policy and foster a community of hope and inspiration for one another.

When we lobby, we are loving our neighbors without exception. We are saying that, even if I don't agree with your positions as an elected official, I will respect you and speak and listen with love. And I can expect the same in return—this is civil dialogue.

Your role as governors and close supporters of this organization offers you a way for your personal witness and for your meeting or your community's witness. FCNL also avails itself to a much broader community of people who share the inward experience of hope and value the dignity of every person. We help set up the opportunities for people to speak about these values and hopes through advocacy.

Undoubtedly, many of you already connect with other people and organizations in your communities that are working for goals that unite with FCNL's—the affiliations of like-minded people who are willing to stand together is another form of power.

It is true that the policies and practices of the Trump administration have accelerated activism—although the problems we are responding to didn't start with this administration. In local communities across the country, people are organizing and working on solutions in ways that empower people to speak for themselves—Dreamers from Tulsa or Tallahassee telling their own stories or people identified with Black Lives Matter telling their stories of the impact of structural racism from Minneapolis or Nashville.

Social media has given everyone the platform to speak for themselves and to organize digitally. This world of instant communication about every shred of political news affects all of us. Some of you here remember the days when FCNL sent mimeographed action alerts and recorded the action alert on a phone message that people could call into. From the yellow Washington Newsletter to action alert emails to Facebook posts, from Tweets to more visual content, FCNL's communications are evolving.

We know that effective communication is key to transforming national policy discourse. The fact that we are recognized as having integrity and expert staff gives FCNL a voice to challenge and change the conventional narratives that guide federal policymaking. We can infuse a clear and distinctive moral, faith-based, and Quaker voice in our educational and advocacy efforts. Using this voice in the media will increase the visibility and reach of FCNL's vision for a just society and a peaceful planet.

The Quaker ethic is not one that boasts or promotes itself. We prefer to be *discovered*. Many of you who are convinced Friends may even tell the story that you were always a Quaker and didn't know it until you took the *Belief-o-matic* quiz on the internet or until you found a local Quaker meeting. As one FCNL supporter recently said to me, "People are looking for you; you need to make it easier for them to find you."

Let me ask you this: How do we stand in the Light and become more visible in a world that amplifies celebrity and outrage and yet hungers for righteousness and humility? What does Quakerism have to offer right now in that world? What does FCNL have to offer now and in the years to come for a political environment that is too often toxic and harsh, an environment that makes those who want to live in peace and simplicity turn away?

We are all called to witness, even if we don't feel capable and even when we feel weary. Elizabeth Fry, a Quaker prison reformer and philanthropist who lived from 1780 to 1845, said, "I look not to myself, but to that within me, that has to my admiration proved to be my present help, and enabled me to do what I believe of myself I could not have done."

When we stand in the Light, the doubts, the fear, the hesitation melt away, and we gain a power that comes from within—a power to speak truth. It is our experience of *truth* that is the foundation of our witness.

It is not driven by political party or political identity; it is bearing witness or doing the truth. As Thomas Gates describes in the Pendle Hill pamphlet "You Are My Witnesses," the testimonies for early Friends were not simply a list of virtues, but were the lived witness of their daily lives—"the outward and visible manifestation of an inward transformation."

When Jesus chose his disciples, he didn't go for the Ivy League grads of his day. He asked the fisherman and talked to the women who others shunned. He paid attention to children. Jesus taught us how to love our neighbors without exception.

Shouldn't we do the same? Shouldn't we talk to everyone? Shouldn't we welcome everyone who is looking for ways to practice hope, to open the possibility of faithful action? Do we have a faith that is alive, a practice that is inspired?

FCNL strives to be led by the Spirit in its work. Friends always have held that spiritual clearness can be discerned in community with fellow seekers. The theological and political diversity and practices among Friends offer FCNL an opportunity to build a stronger Quaker constituency. FCNL has a unique position to engage in peacemaking among Friends and on behalf of Friends. We need one another to do this work.

Friends are often reluctant to talk about the use of power, and while we speak of our "prophetic witness," we don't always define it. Recently, I have been reading Abraham Heschel's book, *The Prophets*, and it has helped me understand something about prophetic witness.

He states that "the main task of prophetic thinking is to bring the world into divine focus." Seeking a world free of war, a society with equity and justice, a community where every person's potential can be fulfilled, and an earth restored is prophetic thinking.

I want to propose to you that our work of being faithful stewards of God's love is to claim the power God gives us. The faithfulness we exercise in our work at FCNL is to fully live in the power we have through our Quaker faith. We can grow and thrive as we expand that power to bring about the world we seek and speak truth.

These aspirations can only advance in the next five years and beyond with a healthy organization. We will be effective stewards for the planning of our financial, personnel, physical, and technological infrastructure. Given the rapid organizational change of recent years, we are strengthening

Standing in the Light: Power, Politics, and Prophecy

our FCNL not only through our Quaker practice but also through effective nonprofit management.

Spend a moment with me imagining the future of FCNL. Imagine if

» we truly claimed the power of standing in the Light: responding to the social, political, cultural changes, that is, being open to divine revelation, while holding to the truth that we know—that God's love in not changeable.

» we practiced "dangerous unselfishness," the Rev. Dr. Martin Luther King Jr.'s admonition regarding support for the striking sanitation workers in Nashville before he was murdered.

» the young adults who connect to FCNL through Spring Lobby Weekend or Advocacy Corps or summer internships or Young Fellows started attending Quaker meetings because they were captured by the welcoming and inclusive communities of our meetings and churches.

» in the next year, every one of the 425 people in this room tonight committed to visiting a district office of your congressional delegation—either your two senators or your representative—every month. That's over 5,000 lobby visits in the coming year.

» when you return home, every one of you found three other people who will commit to taking action online each week—a commitment of 10 minutes a week. That would be 1,275 people times 45 weeks for a total of 57,375 messages to congressional offices every year from FCNL constituents!

» every week that Congress is in session, we have a group of advocates packing the Quaker Welcome Center to learn, lobby, and lead.

» we had not 80 Advocacy Teams in 36 states, but 535 Advocacy Teams—one for each of the congressional districts in this country.

» the Friends Committee on National Legislation had the name recognition of the National Rifle Association or Amnesty International.

» all the members of the House Foreign Affairs Committee and the Senate Foreign Relations Committee called on FCNL to help write new legislation that advances peacebuilding, human rights, and diplomacy.

» the Republican and Democrat leadership of Congress and the administration figured out that a fair carbon tax is a positive solution to the problem of climate change.

» the iconic words on the Statue of Liberty, "Give me your tired your poor, your huddled masses yearning to breathe free," meant that we welcome the stranger to our country—refugees and immigrants.

» we practiced loving our neighbors without exception every day.

We have no small plans for FCNL. If we are successful, we should expect that our work will help people in the United States and around the world feel more secure—from the

Standing in the Light: Power, Politics, and Prophecy

threats of war, climate change, economic insecurity, and the violation of human rights.

We should expect that people who work with FCNL will feel hopeful and experience a renewed confidence in our political system's ability to affect positive change in their lives and the lives of people across the globe.

FCNL has a power to influence public policy in the United States and thereby around the globe. In 1974, our first executive secretary, E. Raymond Wilson, wrote these words that have even deeper resonance today:

> *"Why try to work uphill for peace, justice, and freedom on Capitol Hill at a time when cynicism about the character and operation of government and government officials is widespread and when disillusionment about the church and organized religion is so common and so vocal? Because religion should be vital and relevant and because the health and the future of democracy rests upon responsible participation by informed and concerned citizens.*
>
> *"A world without war, without conscription and militarism has still to be achieved. Even in the United States the price of liberty is still eternal vigilance. The battle for justice is never-ending. A world dominated by military, economic and political power easily forgets fairness and compassion for the disadvantaged and dispossessed at home and abroad.*
>
> *To strive for these and similar goals has been the role of the Friends Committee on National Legislation."*
>
> *– From* Uphill for Peace, *by E. Raymond Wilson*

Leading with Hope, Faith, and Love: The Diane E. Randall Collection

This is what we have done for 75 years; we are doing it day in and day out, through our collective action.

What am I asking of you tonight? Help us grow FCNL's power.

Strengthen our spiritual foundation. Hold us in the Light, every day. If you are a praying person, pray for FCNL—for our General Committee, for our staff, for our Advocacy Teams, for our Visiting Friends, for our Advocacy Corps. Pray for the elected officials we talk to.

If you don't pray, but you meditate, hold us in the lovingkindness of the universe. Wrap us in the good intentions for creating a better world.

Support FCNL financially. If you are monthly sustainer, a monthly donor to FCNL, consider an increase. Did you make a stretch gift to the capital campaign? Consider another special gift to honor FCNL's 75 years. Many of us in this room may miss the celebration of FCNL's 100th birthday in 2043, but your presence will still be felt—through a legacy gift.

Recruit new people to join us. Let your lives speak. When people see how you are empowered by lobbying, it will attract others.

Above all: Speak Truth to Power. Speak of your values and of the moral underpinning that guides your life. Exercise your heart and soul by creating time in your days and weeks for silent reflection and for being present with people in ways that builds community. Speak Truth. Act from Hope. Show Love.

Together, we can work toward that world that we imagine.

Diane presents the Ed Snyder Peace Award to Rep. Keith Ellison (MN-05) for standing against discriminations and protecting international diplomacy with Iran at the Annual Meeting in 2017.

FCNL at 75!

West Richmond Friends Meeting » May 13, 2018 » Richmond, IN

The Friends Committee on National Legislation began at a meeting in Richmond, Indiana, in June 1943. Today, 75 years later, the FCNL Executive Committee thought it would be fitting for us to mark the occasion by returning to the site of our founding, Quaker Hill Conference Center. We have spent the past two days with members of our standing committees in meetings at the conference center, and have held public events at Earlham College, highlighting our history, our current work, and our future.

We have also talked about the political climate and our spiritual condition. This morning I want to talk about how our spiritual condition can impact our political condition and vice versa. I hope this message challenges and encourages you.

The scripture passage I have chosen for today is 2 Timothy 1:6-9, which reads,

> *"For this reason I remind you to rekindle the gift of God that is within you through the laying on of my hands; for God did not give us a spirit of cowardice, but rather a spirit of power and of love and of self-discipline.*
>
> *"Do not be ashamed, then, of the testimony about our Lord or of me his prisoner, but join with me in suffering for the gospel, relying on the power of God, who saved us and called us with a holy calling, not according to our works but according to his own purpose and grace."*

What is your spiritual condition? Do you know your holy calling? Or are you, like me, a little afraid of having a holy calling? In his letter, Paul tells Timothy that the power of God has saved us, called us by grace and for a purpose.

Recognizing the purpose and grace to which God has called us can be intimidating because it means we are going to have to live into it. I remember when I first began seriously contemplating ministry as a Friend. I attended a workshop at Woolman Hill in Massachusetts about 25 years ago on gifts of ministry and eldering with Jan Hoffman.

As the facilitator of this workshop, Jan asked us all to write a description of our ministry in advance and send it to her. I was reluctant to name a ministry because that would be describing a *holy calling*, which felt presumptuous. Ministry felt like something for people who work in churches and who exude goodness and love. (I realize now that if I had gone to Earlham School of Religion and had the benefit of deep and guided contemplation, I would have been better equipped to name ministry.)

I don't remember exactly what I wrote about ministry for that retreat, but it was on the theme of working for justice through political advocacy. At the time, I was advocating for affordable and supportive housing in Connecticut and had no idea that this sense of ministry might lead me to FCNL.

I do remember, however, the new understanding I had for how Quakers think of ministry—that we each have the capacity to minister to one another and that our holy calling comes from God and is manifested in how we live in the world.

Do we live with a spirit of cowardice? Most of us probably wouldn't confess to cowardice, and it's hard for me to even imagine Quaker cowardice. But when I think of the characteristics of cowardice, I think of complacency, avoidance, fear, and despair. I know that our political culture and economic and social conditions can lead us to these conditions.

I have seen it in myself when I think, "I don't need to speak up, show up, or take action because someone else will speak up about the racist remark. I don't need to say anything;" or "I won't know exactly how to explain my support for the Iran Deal if I call my member of Congress;" or, "it won't make any difference if I fast in solidarity with others in the faith community to highlight hunger because no one is paying attention."

But God does not give us the spirit of cowardice, complacency, fear, or despair. God gives us the spirit of love, power, and self-discipline.

For those who feel like the antidote to cowardice is doing everything—being a political expert or a super activist and organizing for peace and justice on every issue—God's spirit of self-discipline only means listening to the holy call. God doesn't call us to exhaustion or guilt. God calls us to power and love. This is not political power, nor is it economic or celebrity power. It is the spiritual power of being grounded in God.

How do we experience worldly power? We are surrounded by it. Worldly power is in privilege from being white; being educated; having wealth; or living in the culture of wealth, celebrity, or media hype. I live and work in a place that oozes with worldly power. The decisions that are made (or, in some cases, not made) in the halls of Congress and in federal agencies affect every one of us in the United States.

Many of those decisions—issues of war and peace, the imperative of a warming planet, the enormous challenge of 60 million refugees around the globe, or the economic and social burdens created by income inequality—also affect people across the globe.

How do we know the power from God's spirit? To me, it looks like loving our neighbors without exception. It's in knowing that each one of us has a holy calling to respond in our own God-given way to the brokenness of our world, our

own communities, and our political systems; to the pain of families impacted by addiction or poverty; to the fear that accompanies joblessness or illness; and to the longing that comes from isolation or emptiness.

The power of God's spirit is manifested when we offer a home to the refugee or the unhoused, when we counter the narrative that militarism is a solution to our fear of others. God's spirit of love is evident when we stand up to the policies and practices of detaining, jailing, and ruining the lives of Black and brown people as a rationale for safety. We know the power of God's love when we see that of God in every person—regardless of religion or nationality.

The power of God's spirit is a fresh incursion of the Holy Spirit, the breaking in of a new understanding that each of us has a holy calling. As the Religious Society of Friends, we have a powerful voice for peace and justice. We can and should speak boldly when we are clear as a meeting or church.

This is not simply a legacy of those Friends who lived before us, participating in the underground railroad and working on the abolition of slavery. It is more than those conscientious objectors of the last 100 years who risked scorn, jail, and loss of work due to their refusal to kill others in war. It is more than those among us who steadily reduce our carbon footprint as both a witness and a pragmatic step to counter climate change.

We, as individuals—as citizens and as people who care about the public welfare and life in our country and around the globe—must be engaged in the political system. Good citizenship is more than voting.

FCNL at 75!

Finally, it is possible through our actions to have an impact. It is possible to, as the Rev. Dr. Martin Luther King Jr. said, bend the arc of history toward justice.

Last December, as I spent time in reflection about the state of the world, I felt some despair, some sense that the arc of the universe had snapped back, much like a birch tree weighted with snow springs back. We all experience this feeling from time to time, whether because of the state of the world or for more personal reasons.

As one whose *holy calling* is to encourage others to act for social justice and to build relationships with political officials, I prayed for the spirit of God that brings love and self-discipline—even amid despair.

In his letter to the Galatians, Paul describes the fruits of the spirit as peace, patience, kindness, love, joy, and self-control. Sometimes, I use this as a checklist. Am I living in the spirit, am I seeing these fruits of the spirit in my life? Note the similarities in Paul's encouragement to Timothy: God does not give us a spirit of cowardice but a spirit of power and love, and self-discipline.

I have learned that there is joy in finding community where we least expect it—in interfaith gatherings, in one-on-one dialogues. There are alternatives to violence practices in prisons, or in international areas of violent conflict. There is love and self-discipline in the midst of despair.

And so, as FCNL begins our next 25 years, we boldly venture forth, rooted in God's love, grounded in Quaker faith and practice, and guided in Light.

Gracious Calling, Ordered Lives:
The Faith and Practice of Friends in the Political Maelstrom

North Carolina Yearly Meeting (Conservative) » July 13, 2018
Greensboro, NC

Six weeks ago, when I was asked to give a title to this talk, the lines in the poem, "Gracious calling, ordered lives," jumped out at me. These words sum up why I am a Friend and why I am devoted to the labor of moving public policy toward peace, justice, and an earth restored. I have experienced the gracious calling of "bold service to the Lord," and I have experienced the ordered life of the Spirit in my practice with Friends.

This beautiful poem by John Greenleaf Whittier offers a sensibility that is pretty much the opposite of what life is like on Capitol Hill in Washington, D.C. The sense I get reading the words of this poem or hearing it sung is one of invitation to rest in the Lord, of "calm," "tender whisper," and "still dews of quietness."

The experience in Washington, D.C., these days is more "earthquake, wind, and fire." I've even heard people describe Washington as toxic. But it is not just in Washington that people recognize a political, social, and cultural gap. Neighbors and families in communities across this country stand in what Parker Palmer calls the "tragic gap." This is why the spiritual practices and disciplines of Friends are so essential in this time and for this work.

The Friends Committee on National Legislation—a Quaker lobby established 75 years ago in the throes of the Second World War—is living into the gracious calling to witness for peace and justice on Capitol Hill. I would like to tell you about the witness of our legislative priorities and of people across the country. I will share how the vitality of the spiritual life of Friends is intimately entwined with the health of FCNL and how we seek to be inclusive, vibrant, and bold, bringing our ordered lives to witness for the world we seek.

> *We seek a world free of war and the threat of war.*
> *We seek a society with equity and justice for all.*
> *We seek a community where every person's potential*
> *may be fulfilled.*
> *We seek an earth restored.*

This bold vision establishes the foundation of the public policies FCNL promotes. From this vision and from your discernment in meetings and churches to guide us, we create a set of legislative priorities for which FCNL advocates at the federal level. Every day we see opportunities for advancing these priorities in Congress. We see how ordinary citizens can develop relationships with their members of Congress that can influence those members. We see how using the media to raise concerns through letters to the editor has an impact on public officials and shapes the public narrative.

Last year, the FCNL network published 290 letters to the editor in 200 different newspapers across the country. FCNL's network and lobbyists visited 948 offices in-district and in Washington, D.C. We know these visits and letters to the editor have an impact because members of Congress and their staff tell us so.

Even when members disagree with us, our efforts to reach them have an effect. Quakers are respected; our practice as Friends brings a way of listening and speaking that is unusual for most congressional offices. We can sometimes offer quiet and balm to the frenzy of political life.

FCNL invests in training and coaching people how to be effective in talking to members of Congress—the people who represent us in that third branch of our federal government. Just as we establish an order for our worship to conduct business, we encourage advocates to establish an order for meetings with congressional offices. We encourage people to tell their stories of why they are concerned about a particular issue and why policy matters to them.

Last fall, I witnessed firsthand the impact our personal stories can have on our elected officials. It was in a meeting with Maryland's Sen. Chris Van Hollen about the urgency Friends feel for Congress to cut Pentagon spending and get a clean audit of the Department of Defense. It was a productive meeting, but the heart of the conversation came near the end, as the senator was about to leave.

Dat Duthinh, a member of the Advocacy Team from Frederick, Maryland, asked to tell his story. As a child in Vietnam during the war, Dat lived the reality of war in a way no child should ever have to experience. He told Sen. Van Hollen he was there to talk about the consequences of spending money on violent destruction.

Speaking about video footage of children in Hanoi, Dat said, "I could have been one of those little boys fleeing the bombing of Hanoi." He looked his senator in the eye and told him, "I hope you can hear that this drastic increase in the Pentagon budget is against the moral values of the people here." It was a powerful moment—and my privilege to witness it.

In our Quaker Welcome Center, a newly renovated green building adjacent to FCNL's office, we provide space for Friends like Dat to attend lobby trainings and events—both in person and, thanks to technology, digitally from their homes. We also host a weekly time of silent worship and reflection. We hold this space for people like Dat and for people like you—Quaker advocates who want to come to the Hill to pray, learn, and share their stories with Congress.

In May, a group of seven from Pittsburgh Friends Meeting traveled to Washington to meet with Rep. Michael Doyle (PA-18) and ask him to co-sponsor the No Unconstitutional Strike Against North Korea Act.

These Friends came to the Hill to voice the peace testimony that Quakers have held in our hearts for nearly 400 years:

> "[T]he spirit of Christ, by which we are guided, is not changeable, so as once to command us from a thing as evil and again to move unto it; and we do certainly know, and so testify to the world, that the spirit of Christ, which leads us into all Truth, will never move us to fight and war against any man with outward weapons, neither for the kingdom of Christ, nor for the kingdoms of this world."

After their lobby visit, the group joined in worship with FCNL staff. One Friend noted that witnessing and participating in FCNL's work firsthand gave him a deeper, fuller understanding of how being a Friend resonates with the work of FCNL.

We live in a time when it is easier than ever to talk to Congress, to speak truth to power. Advocates can travel to see their lawmakers in person, take action over email and social media, and even program numbers into their mobile phones so their members of Congress are just a call away. We see time and again how this engagement inspires hope and empowers change.

At the same time, we are all experiencing the political maelstrom. We know our country and our world are in the throes of dramatic change, fissures that test our politically divided communities and families; inhumanity and white supremacy, both current and historical, that test our democracy; a planet in distress; and over 60 million people displaced from their homes, causing an unprecedented refugee crisis and global upheaval.

Communications platforms have exploded with access to constant and endless information, challenging our capacity to make meaning from this glut of data. Turning off the spigot of social media, allowing for times of coolness and stillness, brings us back to the Center, as Whittier describes. It is our return to the Inner Guide that allows us to be "bold in God's service."

Later this summer, I will be giving the Bible half-hours at New England Yearly Meeting. Their theme, from "Fruits of Solitude," is this: "In fear and trembling, be bold in God's service." In choosing the biblical texts for these morning sessions, I find myself drawn to verses that describe love. In 2 Timothy 1:7, Paul writes to Timothy, "For the Spirit God gave us does not make us timid, but gives us power, love, and self-discipline."

Our efforts to move public policy in Congress can be slow and sometimes tedious. That is one of the reasons we Quakers are good at this. We understand that finding common ground takes time, and we try to listen beyond the words. It requires faith and tenacity to build relationships with elected officials. It's not enough to vote and to think we have done our civic duty; it's not enough to show up for vigils and marches and feel that is sufficient witness.

As constituents, as people who see the possibilities of a more just and peaceful world, we need to be in the offices of our elected officials. We need to talk to them by phone, by email, and on social media. We need to work with our faith partners to show solidarity and numbers, speak to the call of our religious beliefs, and experience that God loves every one of us.

Quaker history is written significantly by our witness to the power of God's love in the political maelstrom. We were founded at a time of foment and dissent. Many suffered imprisonment for defending their religious beliefs. Our Quaker ancestors came to this country seeking religious freedom. From the earliest days, Quakers lobbied and did civil disobedience. A favorite quote of mine is from Friend Edward Burrough, who wrote in 1695,

> *"To the Present Distracted and Broken Nation of England: We are not for names, nor men, nor titles of Government, nor are we for this party nor against the other ... but we are for justice and mercy and truth and peace and true freedom, that these may be exalted in our nation, and that goodness, righteousness, meekness, temperance, peace, and unity with God, and with one another, that these things may abound."*

This is as true today as it was then. Our commitment to justice, mercy, truth, peace, and freedom remains.

Regarding FCNL's peacebuilding efforts, there is a ray of hope passing through Congress that the United States is willing and able to do more to support peace and prevent violence. On June 26, the Elie Wiesel Genocide and Atrocities Prevention Act passed the Senate Foreign Relations Committee with overwhelming bipartisan support. This is a major step toward the peaceful prevention of deadly conflict. After years of hard work, we are so close to seeing this important legislation become law.

One of the breakthroughs in moving this through Congress came when a group of North Carolinians—some here today—visited the office of Sen. Thom Tillis (NC) during the FCNL Annual Meeting in November 2015. The group spoke with the senator's legislative director for foreign policy, a former military person. They were able to convince Sen. Tillis to support the bill, indicating bipartisan support. This was an important step in advancing the legislation.

Now, we are pushing to see this legislation considered on the floor of the House and then the floor of the Senate. Sen. Tillis's role continues to be important. You, as his constituents, can ask him to ensure this bill gets a vote in the Senate.

You can also ask Sen. Richard Burr (NC) to support the legislation when it comes up for a vote in the full Senate. The world continues to know violent conflict and war, but when this bipartisan bill passes, the United States will have taken a step toward better response to and prevention of future atrocities. This will save lives and money.

FCNL Advocacy Teams—small local groups of advocates who use their power as engaged constituents to build relationships with members of Congress—have focused their power on preventing nuclear war with North Korea. The United States has a moral responsibility to use diplomacy and engagement at all levels of government to prevent violent conflict. A war with North Korea would be catastrophic for the Korean peninsula, the United States, and the world.

We welcomed the summit between President Donald Trump and Kim Jong Un in June and hold both leaders in the Light, willing our countries to continue to engage in diplomatic negotiations. Unsurprisingly, there is deep concern over the commitment of these two leaders to understand that diplomacy is a marathon, not a sprint; that achieving the step-by-step political, military, and technical support to execute agreements for denuclearization requires more than a handshake.

We remain deeply concerned that military action is too high on the United States' list of solutions to global conflicts. We are also concerned that Congress is shirking its constitutional authority to debate U.S. involvement in war. Congress does not want that debate. The debacle of the Iraq War was a tragic decision that resulted in more and more people understanding that war is not the answer.

Instead, Congress is willing to allow for "security assistance" and billions in arms sales to other nation states. It is essential for Congress to reassert its responsibility to debate and authorize war to ensure that the president doesn't have unilateral power to take our country into another war. If you agree, I encourage you to talk to your congressional offices.

The outsized military budget that exceeds $700 billion dollars is another sign of this country's dependency on the military industrial complex. There are military contracts in all 435 congressional districts; spending at the Pentagon has nearly uniform support from Congress—sometimes over the objections of the military.

Military contractors have created an insatiable beast in developing more weaponry that is paid for with our tax dollars and exported to countries around the world. In 2017 alone, the United States sold $42 billion worth of weapons to 60 different countries.

This year, FCNL added 51 Advocacy Teams across the country—including two in North Carolina, in Greenville and in High Point. We brought our total number of Advocacy Teams to 98, even reaching Oklahoma and Wyoming. FCNL is recruiting people who share our values and faith in democracy to the cause of preventing war with North Korea.

In this way, we are amplifying a call for peace that sounds around the country. Seventy-five years of witness in Washington, D.C., has shown us that when the people speak their representatives listen.

When New Haven Advocacy Team member Steve Whinfield published a letter to the editor thanking Sen. Chris Murphy (CT) for his support of a bill that would bar the president from a preemptive strike on North Korea, the senator responded by joining FCNL's National Call in March. These relationships are critical to our work. Congress must hear us saying that peacebuilding is the answer, not war.

Let me tell you about FCNL's work to help create a society with equity and justice for all, through our work on Native American concerns. Native American tribes have the inherent right to govern themselves and their lands. This right is affirmed by the U.S. Constitution, by treaties between tribes and the federal government and by court rulings.

Since 1976, FCNL's Native American advocacy program has worked to restore and improve U.S. relations with Native nations so that our country honors the promises made in hundreds of treaties with these groups. The trust relationship between tribes and the federal government—establishing that the United States must treat tribes as sovereign nations and support tribal self-governance and economic prosperity—is also a well-established legal precedent. Yet Congress often ignores tribal leaders' priorities.

The FCNL Native American Congressional Fellow, Lacina Tangnaqudo Onco (Shinnecock/Kiowa), has focused on the issue of missing and murdered Native American women. In some rural communities, Native women face a murder rate 10 times higher than the national average. Despite this, victims in Native American communities are less likely to receive assistance and services.

In 1984, Congress established the Crime Victims Fund to compensate and help victims. Funding for the Crime Victims Fund comes from offenders—not taxpayers—and goes directly to help victims of crime. By setting aside 5% of the fund, amounting to some $220 million in FY 2019, Native American victims can apply for assistance directly.

Next, there's our work on mass incarceration and immigration issues to create a community where every person's potential may be fulfilled. We all lose when we lock people away. Incarceration denies the opportunities for rehabilitation and healing that are necessary for a person to fulfill their potential.

This is a loss—not only to the individual and their family, but to society as a whole. Our communities and families will be strengthened by a system that embraces restorative justice and seeks to return rehabilitated offenders to society with their full rights and obligations.

Incarceration of violent and destructive individuals is sometimes necessary for safety, but community-based alternatives to incarceration are often better responses to nonviolent crimes. A well-functioning system will include equitable and prompt adjudication, education, training, and treatment for those convicted and restitution to the victims of crime.

At the same time, many crimes are prompted by conditions that can best be addressed outside the criminal justice system. Violent acts that stem from using, selling, or transferring drugs or obtaining money to use them should be prosecuted.

However, substance abuse itself is fundamentally a health issue requiring prevention, education, treatment, and rehabilitation. Mental health problems deserve treatment rather than criminalization.

FCNL has lobbied for the Sentencing Reform and Corrections Act (SRCA), which would reduce mandatory minimum sentences in the federal judicial system. This bill stands in contrast to prison reform legislation recently passed in the U.S. House of Representatives—legislation that does nothing to address the problematic, racially biased mandatory minimum sentences that are the root of mass incarceration.

In May, we welcomed Sen. Chuck Grassley (IA) to our Quaker Welcome Center on Capitol Hill to thank him for his leadership on the Sentencing Reform and Corrections Act (SRCA). This bill passed out of the Senate Judiciary Committee this year with strong bipartisan support, despite opposition from the U.S. Attorney General.

The SRCA is an example of what Congress can do when partisan lines are crossed in the name of justice. Now, José Santos Woss, FCNL's legislative manager for Criminal Justice, and our strategic outreach team are urging our networks to ask congressional candidates to support legislation like the SRCA, give judges more discretion in sentencing, and take a step towards lowering the federal prison population.

Sentencing reform is vital to our work for racial justice and our vision of a community where every individual has a chance to answer the Divine call of the Spirit in their own lives. Migrants and refugees also deserve that chance. At our Spring Lobby Weekend this past March, over 400 young adult advocates came to Washington to lobby for immigration reform. They asked Congress to reject proposals for a wall and support protection for Dreamers, their families, and undocumented immigrants.

Vashti Meza, a student at the University of Texas Health Science Center at Houston, came to Washington from El Paso, Texas, to meet with her representatives. To hear Vashti speak was to understand why we must have compassion for migrant families who are seeking to build lives in this country.

To the gathered crowd at Spring Lobby Weekend, Vashti said, "Immigration is a tough subject for me. My father was deported in 2005 back to Mexico. Two years ago he was murdered there. I want to prevent other families from being torn apart like mine."

The energy, intelligence, and commitment of young people like Vashti renews my faith that there is a path toward just, fair immigration reform. I see the light shining in them, and it gives me hope. Despite the voices calling for justice in immigration reform, Congress still has not yet acted on this issue.

This summer we have felt the outrage and heartbreak of U.S. policy to separate children from their families at the border. Recently, Attorney General Jeff Sessions quoted Romans 13:1 to justify the administration's cruel zero-tolerance immigration enforcement. But the full passage restates the teachings of Jesus: "Whatever other command there may be, are summed up in this one command: 'love your neighbor as yourself.'"

This is what I believe: that we are called to love our neighbors—no exceptions. It is wrong and unjust to detain children and families, separately or together, who have crossed our border seeking freedom from the threat of violence. FCNL is lobbying Congress to oppose any legislation that incarcerates children, with or without their parents.

On June 20, World Refugee Day, FCNL asked Congress to uphold its commitment to welcome refugees and individuals seeking asylum. This year, the United States reduced the number of refugees that will be allowed into the country to a total of 45,000—a decrease that is even more shocking in the face of the largest refugee crisis the world has seen since the end of World War II.

Today, almost 1% of the world's population are displaced persons. Congress has a responsibility to right the wrongs of displacement due to war, poverty, and climate disruption. On World Refugee Day, I joined other faith leaders at a press conference calling for an increase in the number of refugees for resettlement to 75,000 in the next year.

The Supreme Court's decision to uphold the president's discriminatory ban restricting Muslims and travelers from seven countries from entering the United States is disappointing and painful—and joins a list of shameful Supreme Court decisions that uphold injustice. From Dred Scott and Korematsu to this ban, the U.S. has a history of enacting cruel policies from behind the shield of legality. But even when they are legal, these policies are wrong.

Mass incarceration, violence at our border, and the Muslim ban together illuminate a painful truth: that Black and brown people in this country face prejudice and systemic discrimination. Many people in communities of color live in fear. We have not achieved the racial justice so many advocates have sought for so long. We must make sure that we carry on the history of advocating tirelessly against unjust and discriminatory policies, as those before us in the faith community have done.

Let me tell you about FNCL's effort to promote an earth restored. It is our moral obligation to address climate change and protect vulnerable communities. Concerned grassroots citizens, along with conservation, business, national security, environmental, and religious leaders, are working to foster a bipartisan and cooperative spirit in Congress to address climate change.

Gracious Calling, Ordered Lives

By changing the dialogue on climate change, we are paving the way for meaningful legislative solutions to gain bipartisan support and become law.

FCNL has been instrumental in helping build the bipartisan Climate Solutions Caucus that now includes 84 members of the House of Representatives— 42 Republicans and 42 Democrats.

This so called *Noah's Ark* caucus requires members to join by two, always one Republican and one Democrat. We do not yet have any members of Congress from North Carolina on this caucus; your help in talking to your members can make a difference. This caucus has not yet tackled major legislation, but it has made small steps in legislation that creates openings for new initiatives to address climate change.

We believe putting a price on carbon is essential to make meaningful changes in reducing carbon admissions, and FCNL has established principles for what carbon pricing might look like. While bipartisan legislation has not yet been introduced, we know that members on both sides of the aisle recognize carbon pricing as one policy tool they could act on. Though we don't know when this will be introduced, FCNL will work to guarantee that the principles of fairness are included.

What is affirmed for me again and again when I listen to Spirit is this: We are all, every one of us, graciously called to serve the Divine. As Friends, we have developed disciplines that offer rich spiritual depth, practiced listening, and pragmatic action for the kingdom of God.

So, the question is this: How will we respond to the world's hunger for spiritual life?

The world is hungry for the spiritual life that is lived both internally and externally. As Friends, this is how we live. Do you in your monthly or yearly meetings have something to offer to that hunger? Do our Quaker institutions have something to offer to that hunger?

My spiritual formation as a Friend came in waiting worship—reading Quaker spiritual writing about discernment, testimonies, and holiness—and participating in the life of a Friends meeting.

I have grown in deep contentment and find nourishment in the silence of waiting worship and truth of vocal ministry. I have seen the power of Quaker witness. I know that people the world over long for the spiritual life and the life of public witness. We are all hungry for the gracious calling of God and the ordered lives of the Spirit. We, as Friends, have this to offer to the world.

I believe FNCL has something to offer to people who are disheartened, despairing, and hurt. We can offer a community of collective action. We can share knowledge and information. We can inspire hope and empower change.

We also need the vitality of monthly meetings and churches and the strength of yearly meetings that send their representatives to serve FCNL. We must also engage those who are not Quakers in FCNL—people who are attracted to us because of our stance and our programs.

We have made an investment in engaging young people from diverse backgrounds to be advocates for peace and justice.

To be a part of this movement, you can do the following:

» Pray for or hold in the Light the work of FCNL, that we may be truthful and clear, that our spirits will be sustained. Pray for people around the globe who are displaced, for those whose lives are exposed to violence every day, for those who live in oppression.

» Lift up the vision of the world we seek. Talk about what a peaceful and just world could be. Tell people why you care about justice, why peace is important to you.

» Model the role of spiritual engagement and democracy. The next 3.5 months are the time to participate in electoral politics. Make a plan to vote, and figure out how you can get other people in your city, town, area to vote—particularly young people. Use the FCNL Questions for Candidates to raise the issues that will lead us to a more just and peaceful future. You can raise these questions in the media through letters to the editor or radio, on candidates' social media, or in town halls or public forums.

» Use your financial resources. Support FCNL or our other favorite organization working for social change with a contribution of money or time.

» Speak up again and again to your members of Congress, your local elected officials, those who are searching. Don't think of engagement as *one and done*. Put the congressional offices on the list of folks you check in with weekly. We make it simple to talk to Congress with FCNL Action Alerts. If you aren't sure, contact us or talk to your local Advocacy Corps folks.

» Organize yourselves. Consider forming or supporting an FCNL Advocacy Team with people in your local meeting and people outside of your meeting. Invite them to worship!

» Take a meeting field trip to Washington. Spend part of your day at the Quaker Welcome Center learning to advocate and going on the Hill. Worship with us. Stay at the William Penn House.

» Believe in and reach out to the young advocates who are working for a world with equity and justice. Send a young adult from your community to Spring Lobby Weekend or encourage them to apply for one of FCNL's young adult programs. Welcome the young adults or others in your community who would benefit from silence and spiritual support. Know that your gracious calling may be tender care, it may be mentorship, it may be following.

» Be inclusive. As much as Quakers have to offer, we can also learn from people across this country who are rising to speak out against injustice. From the Poor People's Campaign to March for Our Lives, from Black Lives Matter to United We Dream, we see people mobilized in public places—at state capitals, in public parks, in congressional hearings and the U.S. Senate Office Building. People are showing up, speaking out, and standing with those who are oppressed. You can be an ally, teach nonviolence, listen, take risks, and learn in ways you didn't know you could.

» Listen for your gracious calling; rely on the ordered lives of our religious calling. Do your part. Know yourself and your gifts. Follow William Penn's advice: "Let us then try what Love will do …. Love is the hardest Lesson in Christianity; but, for that reason, it should be most our care to learn it."

Finally, as E. Raymond Wilson wrote in *Uphill for Peace,*

"Why try to work uphill for peace, justice, and freedom on Capitol Hill at a time when cynicism about the character and operation of government and government officials is widespread …? Because religion should be vital and relevant and because the health and the future of our democracy rest upon responsible participation by informed and concerned citizens."

Quaker Fundraising in Uncertain Times

Quaker Fundraisers Conference » September 30, 2018
Philadelphia, PA

I suspect I was asked to speak partly because FCNL just completed a successful and inspiring capital campaign last year that has strengthened our operations in several important ways, but also because FCNL lives and works in the cauldron of political, cultural, and social upheaval as we lobby for Quaker legislative priorities with the United States Congress.

No question, we are living in uncertain times. You may feel that uncertainty from the perspective of "where will the money come from to sustain our budget" or "to build our scholarship program" or "to put an elevator in our meetinghouse." I believe the uncertainty of these times goes beyond whether there will be a recession or how the new tax law will impact charitable contributions. There is an uncertainty affecting the heart and soul of our democracy, our civic institutions, our faith communities, sometimes even our relationships.

Quakers have a unique and vital role in this time of uncertainty and anxiety in our world. Our history as the Religious Society of Friends was founded and shaped in a time of turmoil. There is a rich legacy of Friends who have confronted injustice, stood for peace, and inspired us through the centuries. They are the forbearers of the Quakerism that is alive today. Our Quaker meetings and institutions will be stronger when we rely on the rich faith and practice that calls us to community and integrity.

Looking around this room, I see professional fundraisers, volunteers, heads and representatives of schools, heads and representatives of Quaker organizations, and representatives of Quaker meetings. I see donors to Quaker meetings, churches, yearly meetings, schools, colleges, and organizations. I also see donors to many other charities. I see a common vocation among all who are in this room, even if fundraising is not directly part of our job descriptions.

My journey as a Quaker fundraiser began when I joined the nascent Development Committee of New England Yearly Meeting (NEYM) about 20 years ago. NEYM had primarily counted on monthly meetings to make contributions although a few individuals also gave gifts.

As the work of the yearly meeting grew and staff were added, there was a need and opportunity to raise funds from individuals. The committee decided to reach out to those who had contributed in the past to thank them and ask why they gave.

I vividly remember the conversation with a Friend from Northampton Meeting who said that giving to Quaker causes was important because Quakers do good work that others don't. I was reminded of a committee meeting at Hartford Monthly Meeting early in the 1990s when we were considering offering a "no interest loan" to the Northampton Meeting as they fundraised to establish a meetinghouse.

Tom Bodine, an elder and Friend in our meeting who had always seemed a bit curmudgeonly to me, was decisive on the matter: Of course we should give this money to them interest-free; we should do everything we could to encourage opportunities for Quaker growth.

The abiding commitment of these weighty Friends to the welfare of the Religious Society of Friends and the spirit of generosity I had heard has stayed with me. It has informed my decisions in how I contribute money and it has given me courage and joy as a Quaker fundraiser.

When I came to the Friends Committee on National Legislation (FCNL), I knew I would be doing some fundraising, but I must have missed part when they said: "we'll be launching a capital campaign soon." Oh, but we did. In its then-68-year history, FCNL had done just two capital campaigns—both of which were instrumental in strengthening the organization in profound ways.

In 2011, it was time to plan for the next campaign. Despite my lack of knowledge, I gained immediate confidence from the overwhelmingly positive results of the feasibility study. The two standout words that emerged were integrity and lobbying. Of course, if you are a Quaker lobbying organization, there are no sweeter words; they indicated that our constituency understands our mission and trusts that we are doing it with integrity.

The other reason that I had confidence in the five-year capital campaign we launched in 2012 was that we hired Barbara Monahan as our associate executive secretary for Development. Barbara's experience and stellar leadership of a dedicated and effective staff has been essential in the campaign and in building an architecture and culture of development at FCNL. Our volunteer Capital Campaign Committee of Friends from across the country guided and grounded our work.

While everyone in this room comes from organizations or meetings that are distinctive in capacity and networks of donors, every organization must have someone who is either hired to fundraise or is doggedly determined to raise the money necessary for operations. Every organization also needs a community of support—a board, a committee who will be cheerleaders and champions, who will themselves be donors and will help tell the story of *why*.

The *why* story makes a difference in giving.

Turning back to the idea of these uncertain times, we do face challenges that are enormously complex and seemingly intractable. Yet, I know that every one of you could tell me a story of hope alive in the face of these challenges.

The first is climate change—the inexorable warming of our planet. No longer just a potential threat, the reality of climate disruption is upon us. The hurricanes, tornadoes, rising sea levels, wildfires, and windstorms all contribute to risks. You are particularly aware of this if your Quaker organization owns and manages property.

Climate change disrupts community life, displacing persons, and catalyzing refugees. Its impacts on the workforce as well as on members of our communities who have physical, tangible, and psycho-social-spiritual needs requires us to confront loss and our fracture with the natural world. It makes me sad when I hear young adults expressing their decisions to not have children because of environmental degradation and a warming planet.

A second major constellation of issues we face is privilege and power that fuels nationalism, militarism, racism, sexism, and other forms of oppression. We see this manifested in our national or local politics. The 2016 election and partisan divides in our country on race, gender, immigration, refugees, and poverty are not just about *us* and *them*. We must hold this mirror up to see our own reflections of how we use privilege and power in our personal and institutional lives in ways that might harm others.

The third is income inequality and the gaping divide between rich and poor. Societies that have massive gaps between the richest members and everyone else often have greater polarization, stress, and chaos. Seven years ago, the Occupy Movement, which some believe was a clear outgrowth of fissures of the 2008 recession, brought awareness to the challenges of having a concentration of wealth in the top 1% of the population. A recent Chicago Federal Reserve study indicates that the income share of the top 1% rose from 15% in 1995 to roughly 22% in 2015.

Quaker Fundraising in Uncertain Times

Now, if your donors are in that top 1% and they love you and want to give their money to you, you may not feel this problem. But if you rely on a broad base of donors to support and sustain your operations, you may be faced with the perceptions of the 99% that they are worse off economically because of this wealth divide.

Lest you think that wealthy progressive people will save us, a new book by Anand Giridharadas, *Winners Take All,* says that wealthy elites reinforce the status quo—regardless of their political perspectives.

These three broad areas represent massive problems that touch us every day—sometimes invisibly and sometimes in a blaring, constant confrontation. We can feel personal despair, dissociation, and isolation when we see racism and sexism so blatantly displayed by people in power.

It is not only in the political arena of Washington, D.C.—the Brett Kavanaugh hearing being the most recent—but also in the use of power and privilege that oppresses *the other* and pervades our society, often in ways that we, who may be in the majority, don't see. Our Quaker organizations and meetings are not immune.

Each of these issues—climate disruption, income inequality, and the abuse of power and privilege—weighs on the work you do as a fundraiser because they weigh on our society. When you are raising money for a Quaker cause, you are not only promoting your program, you are also responding to donors' concerns. Whether it is the meetinghouse that agrees to add solar panels because the meeting is determined to reduce fossil fuel use or the school that convenes a

209

special meeting for worship as a space to respond to high-profile news of racial injustice in order help students make meaning, your organization is acting from Quaker values and testimonies. You have a story to tell about how your Quaker community stepped forward.

Stepping forward to create a better world is what Quakers do, and we do it in a variety of ways: educating children, creating quality of life programs as people age, providing hospitality, offering spiritual refreshment, connecting people across the Religious Society of Friends, and witnessing for social justice. We are stepping forward in ways that nourish the soul and help us to live faithfully in the world.

Parker Palmer describes how those of us who work for a better world stand in the tragic gap—the space between corrosive cynicism and irrelevant idealism. Parker says this:

> *"That's the gap Martin Luther King Jr. stood in his entire life; the gap Nelson Mandela stands in to this day. That's the gap where Rosa Parks and Dorothy Day stood. I call it 'tragic' because it's a gap that will never close, an inevitable flaw in the human condition.*
>
> *No one who has stood for high values—love, truth, justice—he died being able to declare victory, once and for all. If we embrace values like those, we need to find ways to stand in the gap for the long haul, and be prepared to die without having achieved our goals."*

For me, standing in the tragic gap is knowing what is mine to do. I can't fix those big issues I named—climate change, oppression from privilege and power, and income inequality. FCNL and Quakers can't fix those, but we can each be faithful to our gifts and do our part and encourage others to do the same.

I believe Quaker fundraising is different than fundraising for any other organization/cause. We have the spiritual resources of a faith community to ground and surround us. We stand on this history and tradition of Quakers, and we are called to be part of the rich living movement of Quakers today.

I encourage you to connect your fundraising to the living stream of the Religious Society of Friends. In other words, worship. Create spiritual community. Get to know Quakers and those who have built Quaker institutions. Read about them. Learn our history. Tell stories. Build social community that fosters equality and simplicity.

Practice gratitude. Live in abundance. I don't mean simply saying "thank you" for financial contributions and expecting big gifts. Practicing gratitude means we are to give thanks in all ways and truly see the people in our lives—colleagues, donors, family—as beloved children of God.

Walk cheerfully over the earth, answering that of God in every person you meet. Of course, you know this quote from George Fox:

> *"[B]e patterns, be examples in all countries, places, islands, nations, wherever you come; that your life and conduct may preach among all sorts of people, and to them. Then you will come to walk cheerfully over the world, answering that of God in everyone; whereby in them ye may be a blessing, and make the witness of God in them to bless you."*

One aspect of answering that of God in everyone is building relationships. This is fundamental to fundraising and to our work at FCNL. I like to think we practice what Douglas Steere called "Holy listening." *Holy listening* is to *listen* another's being into life. It may be the greatest service that any human being ever performs for another.

We train people across the country in effective advocacy, which starts by building relationships with the staff of congressional offices and the members of Congress. Our lobbyists do the same on Capitol Hill. They aren't simply pushing a point of view; they are listening as well as talking. This is true in our fundraising as well. We see ourselves in relationship with our donors, asking for their support, and deeply listening to their lives.

I have seen how fundraising can be profoundly pastoral. When we talk directly with a donor who has invited us into her home to talk about money, we are invited into friendship. Having a conversation is a way to make a deeper connection to individuals—to talk to them about what they care about, to learn their stories, their concerns, their fears, their hopes. When we approach prospective donors to share our stories and to listen to them, we are acting in right relationship.

When FCNL launched its capital campaign, The World We Seek, Now Is the Time, it was built from discernment the organization had done in 2007 through a committee called the Futures Working Group. Significantly, this group named engaging young adults as a priority.

The 2008 recession and a change in leadership delayed the start of the campaign, but the discernment of that working group that FCNL should prioritize engaging young adults was the central component of the campaign—both to establish an endowment for this work and for current programs.

We also raised endowment for our lobbying and for our Friend in Washington program. Yes, there was a building renovation as well—our new Quaker Welcome Center, adjacent to the FCNL office on Capitol Hill. The Quaker Welcome Center gives us a space for events such as bipartisan dialogues on climate change, meetings with faith leaders and members of Congress on race and poverty, and a weekly time for lobby training and for silent worship.

Finally, I feel blessed to be working at this Quaker organization at a time of uncertainty and chaos to see the deep commitment that young adults bring to the work for justice. My hope for you is that in your Quaker fundraising, you can stand in the tragic gap of these uncertain times, that you know your part to do, and that through relationships with one another and with donors, you are able to see that of God in yourself and in all those you meet.

Tumult, Turmoil, and Truth:
Vital Quaker Witness Today

Stephen G. Carey Memorial Lecture at Pendle Hill » April 1, 2019

Thank you for welcoming me to be a part of the rich tradition of education, worship, and spiritual deepening that is this place. Pendle Hill is as important an institution in the life of Friends today as it has been for almost 90 years.

I speak to you this evening as the head of another important Quaker institution—the Friends Committee on National Legislation (FCNL). We advance effective public policies through federal legislation. That's the heart of FCNL's mission—to build political will for legislation and public policy change that reflect Quaker priorities.

FCNL fields a lobbying team in Washington, D.C., that brings subject matter expertise to congressional offices.

Coupled with constituent voices, FCNL offers a compelling message for peace, social justice, and environmental sustainability by empowering civil dialogue for policy change.

It is my experience in the nearly 35 years that I have worshipped with Friends and in the eight years that I have served as executive secretary of FCNL, that Quakers offer the world a vital faith and practice that is relevant and alive. And Quaker institutions offer depth and breadth to those who hunger for a life in the Spirit.

Quakers and Quaker institutions bring value to the world, a world that is troubled and in turmoil, a world seeking truth. How do we encourage, cultivate, and enable the flourishing of this rich faith and practice to create the world we seek?

Test this in your own life, in the life of your Quaker meetings or in the life of Quaker institutions that you may be attached to. The call of the mission-driven life—the essence of our deep listening for divine revelation, our pursuit of Truth, our practice to let love be the first motion—is essential to who we are as the Religious Society of Friends and for how we show up every day in the world.

In my spiritual formation as a Friend, I learned this practice of inward listening—both individually and corporately. I learned to love my meeting for the space and structure it provided to my religious and spiritual life.

As a convinced Friend, it took some time to figure out how silent worship and vocal ministry worked and how my local meeting related to other Quakers in New England, across the United States, and even throughout the world. But I began to see the value that Quaker institutions bring to the Religious Society of Friends.

I read Pendle Hill pamphlets, attended a Friends General Conference consultation, served on the Advisory Board of Earlham School of Religion, drove my kids and others from our meeting to New England Yearly Meeting retreats, and attended annual sessions. I saw the value these organizations and institutions had and have in my life. I relished the community of Friends, and I learned ways of simplifying by watching and listening to Friends. I saw how Friends let their lives speak, and I knew that I wanted my life to speak to others as well.

Recently, I have been thinking about the communion of saints. It has come to me, more than once and in different places and times as I worship, that those Friends who have died are still present with those of us in waiting worship; that there is a mystical sense of presence as if they inhabit the space. Maybe they only inhabit my heart and soul, their vocal ministry and wisdom still speaking to me.

In the Apostles Creed, which is a statement of belief that binds many Christian denominations in liturgy, the last part—which I recited every week growing up in the Lutheran church—says, "I believe in the Holy Spirit, the holy catholic church, the communion of saints, the forgiveness of sins, the resurrection of the body, and the life everlasting."

Quakers don't have a creed; we don't all believe the same thing, and I'm guessing not many Quakers would agree with that sentence, and I don't either. But I do believe some of it; I believe in the Holy Spirit, the communion of saints, and the forgiveness of sins. For a long time after I became a Quaker I didn't think of sin. Now I do.

In naming the value I see in Quaker faith and practice for confronting the tumult and turmoil of the world, I don't mean to imply that Quakers are the only people who feel a call to a mission-driven life. There are plenty of other people of faith and people who don't profess a particular faith but who are deeply drawn to leading a life from a morally grounded heart and soul.

In fact, one of the joys of my work in Washington is advocating with colleagues on an interfaith basis and recognizing the communion of saints with Muslim, Jewish, Sikh, Buddhist, and Christian brothers and sisters. Together, we realize the possibility of a world where every person is seen as a beloved child of God. Together, we work on federal policies that lead us to that world.

As Quakers, we certainly aren't pure. We don't always experience Divine revelation, and we are sometimes known to be stand-offish, self-righteous, and even testy in our peculiarity.

So, when I say that Quakers and Quaker institutions bring value to the world, to confront the turmoil of the world, I say it as an encouragement and challenge to you; To step fully into who we are and how we are called; to invite others to join us in our Quaker institutions; and to acknowledge that what attracts people to Quakers often is our witness in the world, in living lives that speak.

Stephen Carey was that kind of Quaker. I didn't know Steve, but I have been delighted to read the rich stories of his life in *The Intrepid Quaker*. From his role providing humanitarian relief in Europe following World War II and his acts of civil disobedience in witness, to securing food assistance for millions of poor Americans and his leadership at the American Friends Service Committee (AFSC) and Haverford College, Steve followed a calling for humanitarian service in the world.

Abraham Heschel, the Jewish theologian who wrote about the role of the biblical prophets in the call to social justice, asks, "How shall I live the life that I am?" Over the past couple of years, I have been dipping into Abraham Heschel's book, *The Prophets*, and it has helped me understand something about prophetic witness.

He states that "the main task of prophetic thinking is to bring the world into divine focus." Seeking a world free of war, and the threat of war; a society with equity and justice; a community where every person's potential may be fulfilled; and an earth restored is prophetic thinking.

Last Tuesday on the final day of FCNL's Spring Lobby Weekend, we gathered at a Lutheran church on Capitol Hill for a rousing send-off as the young adults, who had been thoroughly trained and prepped to meet their members of Congress scattered across the Hill to congressional offices to ask for a just immigration policy.

500 young adults from 37 states attended this Spring Lobby Weekend and, over the course of four days, heard from FCNL's colleague organizations who work to end detention, deportation, and border militarization.

They heard from staff in congressional offices about what makes a successful lobby visit, how telling their own stories can be the most powerful way to make the case to elected officials. They heard from FCNL staff—Hannah Graf Evans and Gaby Viera—our lobbyist and program assistant who are our experts leading this issue for FCNL on Capitol Hill.

On Tuesday morning, when Rep. Linda Sanchez of California stood up to address them, she told her own story, how she was the sixth of seven children born to Mexican immigrants; how her parents had limited education, but worked hard to make it possible for their children to go to college and be successful; how her mother, after raising seven children went on to obtain her GED and attend college to become a teacher.

The power of what she said about everyday acts of courage is what resonated for me. Rep. Sanchez spoke about the heroism of Rosa Parks not giving up her seat on the bus and noted how that was a spark.

But the hundreds of Black Montgomery citizens who refused to ride the buses and instead walked long miles to work, to church, or to shop over the course of many months are the everyday heroes of the civil rights movement.

I love that she told that story to the 18- to 25-year-olds in that room, that they may begin to comprehend—from a member of Congress—that it isn't a single action by a celebrity or elected official that makes change. It is the everyday courage of individuals. It is people listening to their Inner Light that guides right action.

In my remarks to these young activists, I encouraged them to use the opportunity of the FCNL training at Spring Lobby Weekend to become effective advocates for lives dedicated to social justice. While a single act can spark change, it is through "the countless actions of individuals who see themselves tied in a single garment of destiny, an inescapable network of mutuality," as Dr. Martin Luther King Jr. declares, that we will make a difference.

Margery Post Abbott's most recent book, *Walk Humbly, Serve Boldly: Modern Quakers as Everyday Prophets*, has given me the encouragement and acceptance to regard my own work at FCNL as prophetic witness. It is not a role that sits easily with me, but Marge's casting everyday prophets as "a people who seek to pay attention to the nudges and visions of the Spirit on a daily (or even minute-by-minute) basis to live in accord with the guidance they receive to help others know this Inward Teacher and Holy Guide"— well, that feels truthful for my own condition.

Are you an everyday prophet? Marge provides further definition: "Everyday prophets are people who are faithful to the path of truth and love and whose lives project hope and a passion for justice. This path is at the core of Quaker worship and spiritual discipline."

Do our institutions, including our meetings and churches project hope and passion for justice? Are we faithful to the path of truth and love?

Do we, in the words of the prophet Micah, "love mercy, do justice, and walk humbly with our God?"

Do we, as Abraham Heschel describes prophets, "bring the world into divine focus"?

People often ask me, "how do you stay hopeful?" Someone asked me last weekend in an even more plaintive way: "Do you see any hope?" I understand why people say this. There are decisions made daily by the governmental power structure in this country and in countries around the world that are a threat to humanity.

People across the globe are being killed in deadly conflict by weapons made in the United States. The U.S. military is fueling Saudi airplanes that are wreaking a terrible humanitarian crisis in Yemen. Civilians are being killed and starved.

What we have known as the existential threat of nuclear war is still with us, and now the threat is renewed with the design of so-called *low yield* nuclear weapons and the $1 trillion price tag for the modernization of a nuclear arsenal in the next decade.

The vision of Shared Security that FCNL and AFSC jointly developed a few years ago is difficult to see in the actions of our country. The president has slammed the door on diplomacy—from decertifying the Iran deal and pulling out of the Paris Climate Accord to ignoring the diligent labor required to advance diplomatic agreements. Witness North Korea. While the opening created by Trump's embrace of Kim Jung Un offered an unprecedented opportunity for North and South Korea, the president walked away from the summit with no apparent deal.

The United States is one of the biggest contributors of carbon output in the world, yet we are pulling back on the commitments we made to the other 190 nations that signed the Paris Climate Accords in 2015 and to families and neighborhoods that have counted on the protections of the Environmental Protection Agency.

Last year, three separate reports issued dire warnings of the growing threat of global warming, eroding biodiversity, and the short time span we have to respond. Yet our Congress resists meaningful action.

At the same time, the administration is radically retrenching through reductions in the federal budget and federal agencies to meet human needs. Our government—of the people, by the people, and for the people—is being twisted to serve a narrow segment of our society, further fueling vast income inequality.

The structural racism built into our public policies over generations that subjugate people with brown or black skin to different standards—from criminal justice to public education to healthcare to housing opportunity— is now more overt with brazen demands and displays from white nationalists.

The grievous acts of white supremacy exhibited in Charlottesville and perpetuated in our border policies today manifest the practices that people of color have experienced throughout their lives—behavior that demeans, degrades, and rejects other than *white*. The fault lines of whiteness that make true equality a lie are deep and touch every one of us.

And now I come back to the problem of sin. These sins—defiling the air, water, and earth; putting human beings in cages; leaving people on the streets to sleep and sometimes to die; spending our governmental resources on nuclear weapons; exporting armaments and violence to countries across the globe; resisting actions to end the scourge of gun violence; hatred, harm and indifference experienced as a reality for too many human beings—are structural sins.

And we are all complicit, even when we do not want to be. These structural or social sins are different than personal wrongdoing, which is how I have traditionally thought of sin. I don't so much think these structural sins are to be forgiven as they are to be recognized as that which distances us from God and is the opposite of holy.

There is a truth-telling in naming this structural sinfulness and injustice that causes turmoil and division to move toward the conditions that foster equality, peace, community, and integrity.

Despite all this—this sin, this turmoil, this trouble, it is easy to wonder whether I see any hope. Yes, I do. In the words of Elizabeth Fry, a Quaker prison reformer and philanthropist, who lived from 1780 to 1845, "I look not to myself, but to that within me, that has to my admiration proved to be my present help, and enabled me to do what I believe of myself I could not have done." So what keeps me hopeful?

New Law to Prevent Violent Conflict

In January 2019, the Elie Wiesel Genocide and Atrocities Prevention Act became law with President Trump's signature. This legislation equips the U.S. government with constructive and cost-effective tools to address the root causes of violent conflict. FCNL led the strategy and lobbying that resulted in the bill's passage in the House and Senate. This success comes after more than a decade of FCNL's leadership to build a strong, bipartisan consensus in Congress for proactive peacebuilding investment.

Yemen: Congress Votes to End Illegal U.S. War

This week the House will once again voted to reassert congressional authority over when the United States goes to war by invoking the War Powers Act to end U.S. involvement in the Saudi-led war in Yemen.

FCNL's advocacy paved the way for the historic bipartisan votes in the Senate and House, educating members of Congress about U.S. complicity in this massive humanitarian crisis, mobilizing grassroots advocates across the country, and leading the faith community's lobbying to end this illegal war.

Criminal Justice: First Step Act Becomes Law

President Trump signed this legislation, the most significant criminal justice reform in years, in December 2018. The new law reduces long prison sentences for nonviolent crimes and improves rehabilitation for those currently in prison. FCNL is a leader in the faith community advocating for criminal justice reform and has worked with our strong grassroots network to persistently push Congress to act to end mass incarceration.

Reauthorization of the Violence Against Women Act Includes Provisions to Address Native American Women's Safety

On March 7, Reps. Karen Bass of California and Brian Fitzpatrick of Pennsylvania introduced H.R. 1585, a bill to reauthorize the Violence Against Women Act, which included provisions that would strengthen the protections for Native women, children, and tribal officers. It expands tribal jurisdiction over non-Indians to include crimes of sexual assault, stalking, sex trafficking, assault of a tribal officer, and child abuse.

These provisions will address the crisis of missing and murdered Indigenous women by improving responses to missing cases through better communication between tribal, state, local, and federal law enforcement. It will also improve data collection and tribal access to federal crime databases. When it goes to the floor for a vote this week, we will be lobbying to keep Rep. Fitzpatrick's and Rep. Bass's protections for Native Americans in the bill.

Gun Violence: House Breaks Barrier on Action

The House's passage of the Bipartisan Background Checks Act in February 2019 is the first crack in the barrier that has prevented any sensible gun legislation from passing Congress for decades. The bill requires universal background checks for all gun sales, closing a significant loophole. FCNL coordinated lobbying of more than 50 faith groups to help ensure this bill's passage.

Here's what else gives me hope: Those 500 young adult participants in our Spring Lobby Weekend—fearless advocates for social justice and peace who bring passion, intelligence, commitment, and love to advocacy—and the 200 young adults who apply to work at FCNL as Young Fellows, summer interns, or Advocacy Corps organizers each year, although we have positions for only 20% of those who apply.

The power of constituent advocacy to influence Congress— FCNL Advocacy Teams, Visiting Friends, Meet-up Motivators, people across the country who are everyday prophets called to act and find a community with FCNL— also gives me hope.

Above all, I am buoyed by the essential hopefulness of waiting worship—of gathering together in expectant listening to the Holy Spirit—and staying open to how this inward experience shapes my outward action.

Spend a moment with me imagining what might be possible through our Quaker institutions. Imagine if

» we truly claimed the power of our faith and practice— to live into the presence of the Divine in the world of turmoil with a radical faithfulness.

» the over 500 young adults who come to FCNL through any of our young adult programs or through Pendle Hill's Continuing Revolution started to consistently attend Quaker meetings because they were captured by the welcoming and inclusive communities of our meetings and churches.

» in the coming year, every one of you in this room committed to visiting the district offices of your two senators and representative—to tell your story, to establish a presence for peace and justice, and to build a relationship.

» every week that Congress is in session, a group of advocates travel to Washington, D.C., and pack the Quaker Welcome Center to be trained to lobby and then go out from our place on Capitol Hill to lobby.

» Congress reclaims its constitutional authority over war and votes to repeal the 2001 and 2002 Authorizations for the Use of Military Force (AUMFs), to pass a no first-use of nuclear weapons act, and to commit to diplomacy and peacebuilding as the most effective foreign policy.

» the Republican and Democratic leadership of Congress and the administration together figure out that a fair carbon tax is an immediate and positive solution to the problem of climate change.

» the iconic words on the Statue of Liberty, "Give me your tired, your poor, your huddled masses yearning to breathe free," meant that we welcome the stranger to our country—refugees and immigrants.

» we practiced loving our neighbors without exception every day.

In 1974, our first executive secretary, E. Raymond Wilson wrote these words that have even deeper resonance today:

"Why try to work uphill for peace, justice, and freedom on Capitol Hill at a time when cynicism about the character and operation of government and government officials is widespread and when disillusionment about the church and organized religion is so common and so vocal? Because religion should be vital and relevant and because the health and the future of democracy rests upon responsible participation by informed and concerned citizens."

This message resonates in 2019 as much as it did in 1974 when it was written, or in 1943 when FCNL was founded. In the same way, William Penn's message from 300 years ago still resonates: "True godliness does not turn men out of the world, but enables them to live better in it and excites their endeavors to mend it."

How do we encourage, cultivate, and enable the flourishing of this rich faith and practice to create the world we seek? How are we speaking truth to power?

As a Quaker institution, FCNL has committed to

» changing public policy to support peace, social justice, and environmental sustainability;

» growing and strengthening our network of grassroots advocates across the country;

» expanding our media and marketing outreach to tell our story; and

» staying grounded in our Quaker faith and practice.

After I had worked at FCNL for only a few months, I had a strong conviction that more people should become Quakers and that more people should know about this organization. I understand evangelism. As I have had the opportunity to get to know Friends across the country and get to know more Quaker organizations and institutions, my belief in what we as the Religious Society of Friends have to offer the world only grows.

Quakers and Quaker institutions—FCNL, Pendle Hill, the American Friends Service Committee, the Quaker United Nations Office, and Quaker schools and colleges to name a few—bring value to the world, a world that is troubled, a world seeking truth. At a time when people are looking to make meaning of the political, social, and cultural turmoil, the moral grounding of Friends can provide a firm foundation.

This Quaker grounding is a place to stand, to build community, to find both challenge and support and renew our spirits, to seek Truth. There is not only one way to Truth, not one way of right action. Steve Carey's ministry was profound and distinct, and his longing to instill the depth of Quaker witness into the institutions he poured himself into deeply resonates with me.

Yet I know that neither Steve Carey nor E. Raymond Wilson nor any weighty Quaker nor any of the communion of saints—the valiant procession of Friends who precede us—not even any of the everyday prophets of today will alone create the world we seek. It is together as we live into that which is holy that we have hope and can love one another without exception.

As Elizabeth Fry says, "I look not to myself, but to that within me, that has to my admiration proved to be my present help and enabled me to do what I believe of myself I could not have done."

Naming the Truths:
Genocide of Indigenous People

November 19, 2019

Sometimes we are touched by Spirit in ways that are both tender and forceful, and we simply can't turn away. Often, these spiritual openings come in places and times that we don't expect.

Last summer, in a meeting with Friends and friends at the First Alaskans Institute, I felt a new opening to understand the sins of my people against Indigenous peoples. The feelings I have experienced—grief, shame, and hope for the resilience of the human spirit—live in me now.

Above: Native American women rally on Capitol Hill, Sept. 11, 2019, for the reauthorization of the Violence Against Women Act. FCNL Photo by Emily Sajewski.

I have felt…

» grief over the grave injustices that have perpetrated generational trauma for Indigenous peoples.

» shame that my white European ancestors and my chosen Quaker faith participated in the cultural genocide of others.

» hope for the resilience of people who perpetrated injustice to ask for forgiveness and for those who have suffered to forgive.

We know of the grievous decisions our government made to deprive Native Americans of their homes on land that wasn't "owned;" to force them to reservations; and to make them compliant to a white, Christian way of being in the world.

In that conversation in Anchorage, what opened for me was to consider how I can be an ally with people who have had their culture, religion, language, livelihood, and families stolen from them. I heard how the actions of those who colonized this land and made it their own profoundly violated the lives of Indigenous peoples. I heard how the effect of those actions manifests in the trauma in subsequent generations.

I heard how the Quakers and other Christian missionaries forbade people in Alaskan villages their dances, their drumming, and their music. This severing of spiritual and cultural practices not only denied heritage, it denied people their stories, denied them the essence of who they are as humans.

The four Friends and the five people from First Alaskans Institute began the meeting with introductions that told our stories. The meeting was led by Ayyu Qassatag (Inupiaq). She named her mother, father, grandparents, home, and language. We introduced ourselves in this way, establishing a personal connection and a space that opened us to one another as humans.

I recognize the value of heart-to-heart conversations as a way for Quakers and other people of faith to listen to and speak the truth of how our ancestors harmed and destroyed Indigenous people and to see one another with respect and love.

I have learned from Friends and from other leaders in Christian churches who are facing the spiritual challenge of confronting how our historic actions have done violence to entire populations based on a false sense of superiority and righteousness. This is essential labor for all of us who are white and Christian.

As I reflect on the meaning of my experience last summer, I have a new understanding of how living in a culture that protects white supremacy and Christian supremacy has affected my way of navigating the world.

It is difficult for the present generation to have to inherit the burdens passed by ancestors, but it feels like a necessary undertaking. I do not know exactly where this opening will bring me, but I am grateful for FCNL's work to address racial injustice—both within the Native American Advocacy Program and in all our legislative priorities—and to be attentive to the inherent racial disparities in U.S. policies.

The work of recognizing injustice, speaking truth, practicing reconciliation is lifelong, and I'm clear that for me it is both personal and policy-focused. Resolution will not come soon or easily, but being available to foster relationships that help us see in new ways creates trust and builds faith that Way will open for healing.

FCNL advocates for legislation that will protect tribal sovereignty and treaty rights. Ruth Flower (center) championed FCNL's Native American Congressional Advocacy Program. She is surrounded by past congressional advocates Lacina Tangnaqudo Onco (Shinnecock/ Kiowa) and Kerri Colfer (Tlingit) in October 2019.

Photo by DAG Photo/FCNL

Fierce Love Now and Forever

October 20, 2020

In these troubled times, it's not surprising that people are anxious, gripped with uncertainty.

Consider this: the COVID-19 pandemic causing over 200,000 deaths in the United States, creating economic hardships and social isolation; tragic wildfires in western states; devastating flooding in southern states fueled by climate change; escalating political tensions; the controversial selection of a new Supreme Court justice; and systemic racism and economic inequality in a sharply divisive campaign season.

As an organization grounded in the faith of the Religious Society of Friends, our policies, priorities, and practices provide a bedrock for these times, a spiritual grounding in God's fierce love.

For Quakers, the inward Spirit fuels outward action. For FCNL, that means we always have a way to exercise faith, hope, and love.

Each day, we practice hope as we advocate. Each day, we exercise faith as we build relationships to create community. Each day—and especially in these times—we know fierce love as we co-create the world we seek.

Hebrews 11:1 tells us, "Faith is the substance of things hoped for, the evidence of things not seen."

Our resolve, our faith to act has never been more important. U.S. democracy is at stake right now.

The opportunity to pursue the aspirations and values we long for—equality, justice, peace, and an earth restored—requires us to act with fierce love.

What does that fierce love look like?

Vote. Talk to people about your values and what candidates you believe come closest to your values. Tell your story as to why voting matters. Tell how you are making sure your vote counts—whether that is voting by mail, early voting, or taking COVID-19 precautions when you go to the polls on election day.

Reach out to candidates. FCNL's questions for candidates provide a resource to talk to candidates running for U.S. representative and senator. Ask their positions. Who we elect is critical—not just for the presidency but for the Senate and the House of Representatives.

Be patient and pursue truth. We recognize that the outcome of the Nov. 3, 2020, election may not be known at end of the day. It may take days or weeks to assure that every vote is counted, as some states do not start counting mail-in ballots until election day. If there is uncertainty of election outcomes, the time between Election Day in November 2020 and Inauguration Day in January 2021 will be tumultuous. The partisanship we see now could become volatile, and our commitment to nonviolence, the rule of law, and truth-telling are ways we exhibit fierce love in the face of lies and extremism.

Advocate with FCNL. At FCNL's Annual Meeting and Quaker Public Policy Institute, November 14–17, we will discern the legislative priorities for the new, 117th Congress. We will also lobby for passage of the George Floyd Justice in Policing Act (H.R.7120). This legislation, which addresses militaristic, racist, and abusive practices by police, is an important bill Congress should pass. Our voices matter in this debate.

Make time for stillness in your life. Pray or ground your intentions in fierce love. Shut out the daily news for a bit and put aside the anxiety, fear, and despair to allow renewal and hope to flourish for the next step of faith.

Fierce Love Now and Forever

This is not the first time that we face the brokenness of our country, of the world. Our spiritual and emotional grounding are essential. In his book, "Healing the Heart of Democracy," Quaker author Parker Palmer reminds us of this:

> *"For those of us who want to see democracy survive and thrive ... the heart is where everything begins: that grounded place in each of us where we can overcome fear, rediscover that we are members of one another, and embrace the conflicts that threaten democracy as openings to new life for us and for our nation."*

And as 1 Corinthians 13:13 reads, "Now faith, hope, and love abide, but the greatest of these is love."

Quakers and all people of faith and moral purpose have a unique and vital role in this uncertain time. Our history as the Religious Society of Friends was founded and shaped in a time of turmoil.

The rich legacy of Friends, who through the centuries have confronted injustice and stood for peace, continues to inspire us today as do the voices of millions of people across the country who are standing, marching, praying, and advocating for justice.

We know we are not alone. Millions of people in this country and around the globe are practicing fierce love by embracing the hope of a world at peace, by working with faith for communities that are just.

A New Season of Hope and Opportunity

December 22, 2020

> "[T]hat's what FCNL has been bringing: a clear moral voice for change to live up to our highest ideals. It's admirable; it's necessary; and it's the time for it right now in the season of optimism, of hope … for the next few years in our country."
>
> — Julián Castro, former secretary of Housing and Urban Development, during the 2020 Quaker Public Policy Institute

For many, 2020 has been a year of anger, despair, and uncertainty as we try to make meaning of this devastating pandemic and polarization in the United States. It has been a year when national political leadership was sorely needed and, too often, was absent or malicious.

We are so ready for leadership that puts people first; leaders who speak truth to confront the global challenges we face—from COVID-19 and climate change to economic and racial injustice and war and the threat of war. We are ready for a time of optimism and hope.

Over 300,000 people have died from COVID-19, and tens of thousands more will die. Yet there is hope—in science and in the vaccines that have been rapidly developed and are already in use. There is hope in the certain knowledge that our lives are connected to the lives of people across the globe. This has a bearing on all the challenges we confront.

We saw Congress respond quickly on a bipartisan basis in March with the CARES Act, pouring billions of dollars into the economy and into the hands of our neighbors who needed help.

You were part of the lobbying for that relief bill.

You continue to participate in our persistent lobbying for the U.S. Senate to act on another desperately needed pandemic relief bill. This will provide unemployment benefits, food assistance, rent relief, and much greater stimulus to local, state, and tribal governments as they respond.

Your continued faithful advocacy has also been vital to the following efforts:

Confronting Police Abuse

In 2020, George Floyd, Breonna Taylor, and Ahmaud Arbery were the most visible among hundreds of Black people who died at the hands of the police. They represent a chilling reality of state-sanctioned violence against Black people that is part of our country's legacy and which continues to this day.

Watching the video of George Floyd's murder awakened people. For many of us who are white or who had been cynical about change, this injustice and the ensuing Black Lives Matter protests brought a renewed commitment for action to dismantle systemic racism.

We joined many coalition partners in advocating for police reform—specifically the Justice in Policing Act (H.R.7120/S.3912). This passed the House of Representatives in June, although the Senate has yet to act on this important bill.

More than 600 of you from 44 states virtually lobbied 80 Senate offices and 151 House offices, meeting staff and members of Congress during our Quaker Public Policy Institute in November. This was the largest turnout of lobbyists on a single FCNL legislative issue. We will persist in lobbying for this legislation in 2021.

A New Season of Hope and Opportunity

Addressing Injustice toward Native American and Indigenous People

We also responded to the generations-long systemic injustice on our Native American sisters and brothers. FCNL has advocated in solidarity with Native American organizations to urge Congress to address the Missing and Murdered Indigenous Women (MMIW) crisis.

With the help of your sustained advocacy, Congress passed two bills to correct such injustices: Not Invisible Act (P.L. 116-166) and Savanna's Act (P.L. 116-165). We will persist in the next Congress to advocate for tribal justice provisions in the reauthorization of the Violence Against Women Act.

Standing Up for Democracy Under Siege

Democracy continues to be a work in progress as we live up to our country's founding principle: all people are created equal. This year, we have seen efforts to deny access to voting and efforts to discount votes.

This suppression and distortion go beyond political polarization. The seemingly endless divide challenges national unity and purpose. And yet, a record-breaking 161 million people voted in the 2020 elections.

At FCNL, we will persist in building our civic education and engagement programs with young adults and people across the country—not only to vote, but to advocate with their members of Congress.

Reclaiming Constitutional Authority for War

We educated congressional offices and advocated with Congress to take back its constitutional power to declare war, which had been ceded to the president in 2001 and 2002. We advocated for repealing these outdated authorizations for the use of military force, in use for almost 20 years, to sanction U.S. military actions across the globe. We will persist in advocating for repeal.

In February, Congress, for the first time, invoked the Vietnam-era War Powers Act to block military action against Iran. Although the president vetoed it, this vote put Congress on record against going to war with Iran and against executive authorization of such a war.

As the 117th Congress starts on Jan. 3, 2021, we are entering a new season of hope and opportunity. With the new

FCNL's Washington DC Advocacy Team joined up with Common Defense for a Rally to Repeal the 2002 AUMF in March, 2021. Photo by DAG Photo/FCNL.

FCNL program assistants Parissa Joukar, Alicia Cannon, Alex Frandsen, and Don Chen. Photo by Emily Sajewski/FCNL.

administration of President-elect Joe Biden, who will be inaugurated on Jan. 20, we will see movement on many FCNL legislative priorities.

However, changes in public policy to make our planet sustainable, to end and prevent war, to build peace, to dismantle systemic racism, to create opportunities for immigrants and refugees—these will require your determined passion and advocacy to create a better world.

Speak truth, act from hope, show love. Together we can work for the world we imagine.

Photo by Brian Feinzimer/FCNL

Impeach Trump

January 12, 2021

Donald Trump must be impeached—for the second time. He and his allies, including members of Congress, must be held accountable for inciting white nationalists and extremist supporters to revolt and try to overthrow the duly elected 46th president, Joseph Biden.

Even as the Jan. 6 events continue to be investigated, and the consequences debated, the fact that President Donald Trump refused to accept his loss in the Nov. 2020 presidential election and that he incited his followers to use force against Congress to prevent the certification of the election is seditious and treasonous. The U.S. Constitution is clear on this as basis for impeachment.

On Jan. 7, we called for Vice President Mike Pence to remove Donald Trump as president using the 25th Amendment. However, Pence has failed to do so, even when Trump's supporters called for him to be hanged as he presided over the counting of the Electoral College votes in Congress.

As Quakers, we do not come to this conclusion easily; neither do we take joy in calling for Trump's second impeachment. We supported Congress's first effort to impeach Donald Trump. Our call for the second impeachment of Donald Trump stems from the same core belief:

> *"We hold our government institutions and officials to rigorous ethical standard of fairness, honesty, openness, and avoidance of even the appearance of conflicts of interest. We expect our government to abide by the U.S. Constitution, national and international law, and international treaties."*
>
> *— "The World We Seek," FCNL Policy Statement, 2019*

Donald Trump and his supporters in Congress must be held accountable for fabricating and perpetuating the lies of a stolen election and using their positions as elected officials to incite an attack by a mob on the U.S. Capitol, members of Congress, and all who worked there as they stormed the building, causing mayhem and terror.

The baseless lies by Trump and his allies, who have used violence to promote white Christian nationalism, is a desecration of the Christian faith and of our democracy. As people of faith, we seek a society with equity and justice for all and where every person's potential might be fulfilled.

That can only happen when we respect the inherent dignity of every person. Racism, misogyny, and religious bigotry have no place in our society or our political life.

White supremacy cannot be ignored for the sake of unity or expediency. To do so will only be to allow these underlying causes to fester and gnaw on the foundations of our society, our democracy. We cannot unify the country until the forces of racism and white supremacy that undergird Trump's and his allies' influence—and which they have summoned to attack Congress—are eliminated. If not, they will continue to tear at the fabric of our common good.

We yearn for a government and a country where civil discourse and civic engagement create the framework for addressing the injustices in our communities and our nation; where all people can act on the courage of their convictions for justice and equity, and we work to make this possible.

The mission of the Friends Committee on National Legislation is to influence federal policies to create a world free of war and the threat of war, a society with equity and justice, communities where every person's potential may be realized, and an earth restored. Making progress towards these goals require all of us who live in this country, especially our leaders, to conduct ourselves responsibly and courageously in the service of the greater public good and our democracy.

As people of faith, we support this second impeachment of Donald Trump and holding his allies accountable. No one, not even the president and his allies, should be above the law.

Photo by Brian Feinzimer/FCNL

Insurrection

February 12, 2021

FCNL urges the U.S. Senate to convict former President Donald Trump of violating his oath of office in this second impeachment trial.

In the waning days of his presidency, Donald J. Trump perpetuated a lie about the outcome of the 2020 election and incited his followers to act out with hate, causing death, mayhem, destruction, and trauma in the Jan. 6 insurrection at the U.S. Capitol.

Trump must be held accountable and never be allowed to hold public office again.

As Friends, we denounce all violence, and we uphold that the peaceful transition of power is essential to a healthy democracy. The extremists who interrupted Congress and wreaked havoc on the U.S. Capitol had been encouraged by the former president over many weeks to prevent Congress from certifying the election.

During the current trial, the House managers have displayed videos that soundly establish the case that Donald Trump is guilty of "incitement of insurrection." Trump's own words, and those of people in the mob who violently broke into the Capitol, establish the links between the former president and the insurrectionists.

The videos assembled for the case demonstrate the grave peril that everyone in the Capitol faced on Jan. 6. We have seen how our legislators and their staff narrowly escaped violent capture—some of them by mere footsteps—as they presided over the certification of electoral votes. The *pro forma* process made official what the public already knew: that Trump had lost the election.

The insurrection was clearly an assault on U.S. democracy, encouraged and abetted by the former President. This impeachment trial of Donald Trump should result in conviction by every senator who believes in democracy and the rule of law. That Senate Republicans would vote against Trump's conviction is a sign of misplaced loyalty.

Leading with Hope, Faith, and Love: The Diane E. Randall Collection

The insurrection was a traumatic inflection of the Trump presidency that encouraged and gave cover to white nationalists throughout his term, to people whose racist, anti-Semitic actions and attitudes have no place in a civil and moral society. Abetted by his supporters, Trump fueled their growth with lies and hate speech throughout his presidency.

The evils of white supremacy cannot be ignored for the sake of unity or expediency. To do so will only allow these festering evils to continue tearing the fabric of our common good. All of those who participated in the violent Jan. 6 insurrection must also be held accountable. Our democracy will continue to be at risk until we create a society with equity and justice for every person.

Our democracy is governed by the rule of law, and we recognize that adhering to the rule of law promotes justice. We cannot have peace or unity without justice. The world we seek requires us to pursue truth. It requires us to recognize that of God in every person and to work for a world where every person's potential may be fulfilled.

As people of faith, we support the second impeachment of Donald Trump, holding him, his allies, and the insurrectionists accountable. No one, not even the president, should be above the law.

Photo by Brett Sayles/Pexels

Stop the Violence Against Asian Americans

March 19, 2021

The escalation of hate crimes against Asian Americans in the United States demands action. No one should be a victim of violence and oppression. The recent murders of eight people in Atlanta, including six Asian Americans, is heartbreaking. Along with millions of people across the country, we mourn the loss of these lives and hold their families and community in the Light.

As Quakers, we denounce these killings, this violence, this xenophobia, and this racism. We must examine ourselves and acknowledge the roles that people of faith, our government, and our institutions have played in perpetuating this racism.

The mass killings in Atlanta are but the latest in the rising violence, xenophobia, and racism against Asian Americans, made worse by lies the former president perpetrated about the spread of the COVID-19 pandemic.

Since March 2020, research by the nonprofit Stop AAPI Hate confirms nearly 3,800 reported hate incidents against Asian Americans and Pacific Islanders. Community experts say that the total number is much higher.

A new study of police statistics from 16 major cities reveals that hate crimes against Asian Americans surged 149% in 2020 while the general average dropped by 7%. Researchers at the Center for the Study of Hate and Extremism at California State University, San Bernardino, which conducted the study, say that a significant number of these hate crimes are against women.

Throughout our country's history, Asian Americans have been subject to racism and white supremacy. Chinese and Filipino people were brought to the United States as cheap labor—and then subjected to violence, like the Chinese massacre of 1871 in Los Angeles, and to laws like the Immigration Act of 1924, which excluded Asians. During World War II, Americans of Japanese descent were incarcerated in prisoners of war camps.

As we seek a world free from violence, we need to root out xenophobia and racism. We should also stop spreading the myth that Asian Americans are *model minorities*, because this myth is often used to belittle other underprivileged people and communities of color.

As we grieve the women who were recently killed in Atlanta, we also hold in the Light the millions of Asian Americans and Pacific Islanders who have been massacred, discriminated against, and subjected to racism throughout our country's history.

Keppler, Udo J., *From the Cape to Cairo*. N.Y.: J. Ottmann Lith. Co., Puck Bldg. Photograph. Retrieved from Library of Congress.

How Can Quakers Dismantle the Racism-Militarism Paradigm?

August 7, 2021

"Take heed, dear Friends, to the promptings of love and truth in your hearts." — George Fox, 1656

For many of us who are Quakers, we have held the peace testimony as an article of faith. It is a basic tenet of our approach to the world—to shun violent conflict and war, to pursue peace, and to order our lives based on the promptings of love and truth in our hearts.

It is not only Quakers or the historic peace churches that shun war. We are joined by millions of people who see the devastation of war and violence and the fallacies of the very foundation of militarism that perpetuates the myth of military might as security.

Quakers also practice a testimony of equality—to answer that of God in every person. We shun racism, antisemitism, sexism, and homophobia. Many of us who are European-Americans struggle to see how white supremacy is baked into our society—into policies that affect our health, education, housing, and public safety and the U.S. approach to international policy.

As Quakers, as people of a faith, how do we regard the racism-militarism paradigm that undergirds our country's foreign and domestic policies? Is this a spiritual concern or an activist concern? How have we adapted our lives in ways that accept militarism and tolerate racism?

Over the past year, as I participated in the discussion group on the *Dismantling the Racism-Militarism Paradigm* project, the idea of prophetic witness was foremost in my mind. It was not a religious or spiritual discussion group—even though some of us are led by faith to confront these twin evils.

But the discussions opened up truths about our history, systems, and the stories we perpetuate about what makes us secure. Yet the reality of the pandemic, climate change, and violence—which wreak havoc—demonstrates a different reality of security.

We are in a time when each one of us is challenged with naming and confronting the broken social, political, and economic systems that deny basic humanity and that deny God's love for every human being.

The paper, "Dismantling the Racism-Militarism Paradigm," by Diana Ohlbaum and Salih Booker, is a result of dynamic discussions among the dozen people on the front lines of confronting militarism and racism.

It offers a prophetic call to confront the root causes of war, policing, immigration policies, and environmental policies. It questions the narrative of security and the trust and acceptance our society and political system has consented to.

These are not only policy or political problems looking for solutions, but they must also be considered and confronted as moral, ethical, spiritual questions for each of us and for us as Friends.

Many Friends are activists, compelled by injustice to act for justice, motivated by devastating climate change to act for carbon reduction and environmental protections. This is how FCNL was founded; Friends gathered to create an organization to have a voice with Congress.

Today, 78 years later, we consistently use our voice to call on Congress to take steps to end militarism and racism— both in our domestic and foreign policies.

It was in an April 1967 sermon that the Rev. Dr. Martin Luther King Jr. called us to see the triple evils of racism, militarism, and materialism. He called for our country to be transformed "from a thing-oriented society to a person-oriented society."

The call continues to be echoed today by the Poor People's Campaign—led by Rev. William Barber and Rev. Liz Theoharis. The campaign is engaging thousands of people across the country in public witness for a moral revival, a Third Reconstruction.

We consistently ask ourselves *What more can we do? How can we prompt a bigger conversation about dismantling the racism-militarism paradigm?* We ask the FCNL community to join us and our colleagues who have renewed this prophetic call.

Consider the discussion paper in your meeting or church. Engage in a discussion with community groups. Consider our own narrative for security and how we can change the narrative to dismantle the systems that do not put all of God's humanity first.

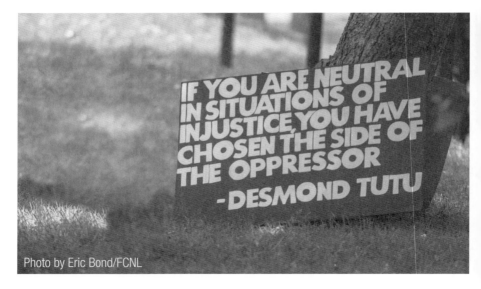

Photo by Eric Bond/FCNL

Our Commitment to Diversity, Equity, and Inclusion

August 10, 2021

The Friends Committee on National Legislation (FCNL) seeks a society with equity and justice for all. How does that translate into our legislative priorities and into the organizational culture of FCNL? How do we live into that vision and become an anti-racist organization?

The reality of white supremacy embedded in our nation's history and still dominant in our culture today affects all of us, but the direct lethal consequences felt by Black people and other historically marginalized people must be recognized and changed.

White supremacy manifests at the personal level in our interactions with others and throughout federal policies that institutionalize the oppression of Black people, Native peoples, other peoples of color, and women.

FCNL has consistently lobbied for changes to these federal policies. In the last few years, our legislative priorities—established by our General Committee—have called on us to "identify, expose, and work to eliminate institutional racism, institutional sexism, and other forms of systemic discrimination."

For those of us who are white and working in a majority white organization, we might assume that because of our commitment to equality, peace, and justice that we are free of bias or oppressive behavior.

However, we know we have much work to do to eliminate bias to become more diverse, equitable, and inclusive. We have much work to do to become anti-racist. Rooting out discrimination and establishing equity requires a conscious and constant effort.

Over the last 50 years, FCNL has offered trainings, held discussions, and considered what we could do to address racial discrimination as an organization. From the 1960s onward, our policy advocacy has included legislative priorities for civil rights and tribal sovereignty.

Six years ago, FCNL staff began a process to address diversity more intentionally within our own organization. We defined diversity across a wide variety of personal identities, backgrounds, and experiences. We adopted a

Diversity, Equity, and Inclusion (DEI) statement and a plan affirming the value of diversity to the wellbeing of FCNL.

The DEI plan created priorities to recruit, hire, and retain staff and program participants who are diverse and to cultivate a culture in which diversity, equity, and inclusion thrive.

As we were expanding our Young Adult program, we recruited from communities that would bring participants who are more representative of our country than the current composition of FCNL's governance or staff.

This includes the participation of young adults who are Black, Indigenous, people of color, and white; who are Quakers, Muslims, Christians, Jews, and *nones*; who are LGBTQ and straight; who come from low-income households and households of wealth; and who attend elite colleges and community colleges. This diversity creates a vibrancy and opportunity for FCNL.

In February 2020, our Executive Committee approved a statement that committed the governance of FCNL to engage in promoting DEI more actively as an organization, including addressing our own behavior and actions that rest on white privilege.

We are now embarking on a new initiative that commits our staff and governance to do the work of justice more justly, with Freedom Road, a firm with experience in faith communities and nonprofit organizations.

Over the next 18 months, Freedom Road will work with FCNL staff and governors to close the narrative gap between the stories we tell about ourselves and the changes we can make to build our capacity as a diverse, equitable, and inclusive community.

We are listening in new ways to those within the organization who have experienced oppression and considering what a racially healed FCNL will be. I am grateful to see the enthusiasm of FCNL to embrace this challenging and necessary work.

With partner organizations here in Washington, D.C., and Quaker communities across the country, we are tapping new resources and sharing experiences on the soul-changing effort to become anti-racist.

We are committed to instituting practices to transform behaviors and attitudes that foster discrimination and inequity.

We are committed to living into our vision of a society with equity and justice for all—as an organization and in our mission to advocate for justice and peace.

As Billionaires Grow Richer, Children Go to Sleep Hungry

Religion News Service » September 27, 2021

The devastating COVID-19 health crisis has become an economic crisis for millions of people— but not for everyone. Last year, families across the United States struggled to put food on the table and balance the responsibilities of childcare and work (assuming they still had a job), but the wealthiest people in our country only got wealthier.

That wealth has not trickled down to families who are struggling to pay their rent, feed their children, and create an economically secure quality of life.

Above: Diane and Rev. Dr. William J. Barber II, co-chair of Poor People's Campaign, join together before a July 2017 rally for healthcare at the FCNL offices.

The American Rescue Plan—the COVID-19 relief bill passed in March—expanded eligibility for two of the most vital anti-poverty programs we have. It made the Child Tax Credit fully refundable, fixing the gap that excluded families in poverty from receiving the same benefits as their higher-earning counterparts.

It also expanded the Earned Income Tax Credit for workers without children, young workers ages 19-24, and older workers over age 65.

Both adjustments put more money into the pockets of low-income people who were previously ineligible—many of them frontline workers in the pandemic. But these payments will expire on December 31 if Congress does not extend them.

These tax credits work, and, not surprisingly, they are wildly popular. The Child Tax Credit provides a lifeline of economic support to families nationwide who need money to pay for daycare, groceries, utilities, rent, and health care bills that pile up nonstop.This is money being pumped back into local economies coast to coast right now, creating a virtuous economic cycle of helping people in need and local business.

Recently, I spoke with Barbie Izquierdo on the value of programs like these. An advocate and consultant who eloquently gives voice for food justice based on her personal experience, Barbie told me that despite all her work—sometimes full time, sometimes part time, often working more than one job—she "would still come home to an empty fridge."

Her story is shared by hundreds of thousands of families across our country.

To this day, the tax credits are one of the primary barriers keeping Barbie from falling back into poverty as she raises her 14- and 16-year-old children as a single mother.

"[They] help you catch up and it alleviates some of the burden of being reminded that you're poor. They've definitely helped me on many occasions," she explained. "Who knows if I would be here today if I didn't have that help?"

Since July, millions of families have been receiving Child Tax Credit checks each month. The latest government data indicates that these robust federal programs have put a dent in poverty, which has cascading benefits for children now and in their future—if we can keep these programs in place past the end of the year.

As Congress continues to negotiate additional recovery legislation, we have a historic opportunity to permanently invest in the future of our children. Congress should seize this moment to not only give immediate help to tens of thousands of their constituents but also to strengthen our country's future.

Specifically, we must adjust the tax code that bends over backward for the extremely wealthy while treating those who struggle every day to afford food and housing as a burden. The more Congress can raise in revenue, the bigger the opportunity we have to address poverty and hunger while investing in our children.

It takes real political will to require corporations and the wealthiest among us to pay their fair share. But we expect nothing less.

As a Quaker, my faith and practice encourage me to treat every person as a beloved child of God, which means I am called to do all I can to foster a more equitable, ethical world in which every person can flourish.

I believe Congress wants to help families in need, to ensure a better world for all. This is their opportunity to support the full refundability of the Child Tax Credit. This is the political moment when we can make transformational change in our country.

Photo by DAG Photo/FCNL

U.N. Climate Conference Underscores Need for Bold Action in Congress

October 27, 2021

The 2021 United Nations Climate Change Conference (COP26) is set to kick off this weekend, and the stakes couldn't be higher. As Friends, "we declare that humankind must respect the ecological integrity and sacredness of the natural world.

Our commitment to the health and well-being of the earth is based on the conviction that there is that of God in all of creation, not just the earth's human inhabitants."

The climate change summit, to be held in Glasgow, Scotland, Oct. 31–Nov. 12, will give world leaders a chance to chart a new future together, one in which care for the planet comes before nationalism and profits. It is an opportunity we cannot afford to miss.

The warning sirens for catastrophic consequences of climate change grow louder and louder. Last August, the Intergovernmental Panel on Climate Change released a devastating report which U.N. Secretary-General Antonio Guterres described as a "code red for humanity."

Another recent U.N. report noted that greenhouse gas emissions hit record levels in 2020 despite pandemic lockdowns, and warned that the world was "way off track" in meeting emission goals.

Meanwhile, wildfires, heatwaves, and record-breaking floods continue to ravage homes and habitats across the world. These words from twentieth-century Quaker Elizabeth Watson echo more clearly than ever: "Only when we see that we are a part of the totality of the planet, not a superior part with special privileges, can we work effectively to bring about an earth restored to wholeness."

World leaders must absorb and act upon that understanding. But responsibility for addressing the climate crisis doesn't just lie with heads of state. If we truly hope to address both the causes and the destructive impacts of climate change, then we need action from the national, local, and individual levels.

Some faith communities and industries have provided leadership for real change through commitments to reduce carbon and their demand on fossil fuels.

However, with the United States positioned as one of the world's highest emitters of carbon, it is imperative that the U.S. administration and Congress take responsibility for the crisis we face. Bold action must be taken to transform our reliance on all harmful energy sources and pollutants that are accelerating climate change and environmental degradation.

Congress needs to pass legislation to reduce carbon emissions. A first step should be a price on carbon, which could rapidly lower greenhouse gas emissions and put the United States on a path to a low-carbon economy that benefits all people. But a carbon tax alone is not sufficient.

Lawmakers also need to place environmental justice at the center of its environmental agenda. The starkest effects of the climate crisis will disproportionately impact low-income communities and communities of color. Congress has a moral obligation to center those most profoundly affected in every piece of environmental legislation it passes.

For Friends, this moment provides a chance to live our faith in action. A recent statement from Quakers in Britain put it well: "Quakers cannot and will not stand by and see everything we love destroyed. We know COP26 will not deliver climate justice—this is a long struggle. But when we take action together, we are powerful, and we are part of a mass movement of people that will not be defeated."

If you're interested in lifting calls for an earth restored, learn more about Quaker Earthcare Witness, a large network of Friends focused on empowering Spirit-led action on environmental concerns. We also urge you to join an Oct. 31 event hosted by the Friends World Committee for Consultation, which will bring together young Quakers from around the world to share their experiences with climate change.

FCNL also has ways for you to act. Take a moment to contact Congress in support of urgent action on climate change. Stay up to date on what is happening in Congress by subscribing to Inside the Greenhouse, our monthly newsletter, or by joining our monthly Call to Conscience. Your lobbying and your voice as a constituent can and will make a difference.

No single gathering by the United Nations will solve the climate crisis. But we pray that COP26 will serve as a global moment of unity and hope that it inspires U.S. political leaders to tackle this grave problem faced by humanity.

Photo by Wesley Wolfbear Pinkham/FCNL

What 20 Years (and Counting) of the War on Terror Must Teach Us

Religion News Service » November 1, 2021

Late on Oct. 7, 2001, less than a month after the 9/11 attacks, American fighter jets swept over Afghan skies. This moment marked the opening of the war in Afghanistan, and more broadly, the beginning of our "War on Terror."

As the fighting began, peace advocates across the world knew what lay ahead. As with any war, there would be needless deaths, horrific destruction, and terrible tragedies.

But few among us could have known the full scope of what was to come. For the next 20 years, the United States engaged in what would become the longest war in our history—longer than the Civil War, World War I, and World War II combined.

The global war on terror has involved dozens of other nations, and over the course of the post-9/11 wars, more than 929,000 people have died, and 38 million people have been forced to flee their homes—all at a cost of more than $8 trillion taxpayer dollars.

Twenty years on, with American ground troops freshly removed from Afghanistan, this is a prime moment to consider what the past two decades of violence have wrought. Given the experience in Afghanistan, it's clearer than ever the global war on terror has been an unmitigated humanitarian and strategic disaster. It is now the duty of our lawmakers to ensure we learn how to prevent and end wars.

War Harms All of Us

As Quakers, we are guided by our faith to pursue a world free of war and the threat of war. This belief is rooted in the obvious fact that war causes unnecessary death and destruction. In the case of the war on terror, this suffering has largely fallen on the shoulders of the people in Afghanistan, Iraq, and other Asian and African countries.

But the endless wars have also brought considerable harm here at home. As the government poured trillions of dollars into the war machine, numerous other pressing issues remained unaddressed. The climate crisis worsened, income inequality sky-rocketed, poverty, and hunger carried on at unacceptably high rates.

Meanwhile, our annual military budget has ballooned to more than $750 billion this year. Even if that figure just holds steady over the next decade (which it rarely does), we will be spending more than twice as much on the military as it would cost to fund the 10-year Build Back Better recovery proposed by the Biden administration. And that was before the $3.5 trillion recovery program began to be drastically scaled back.

Photo by Eric Bond/FCNL

These costs of war aren't as visible, but their impact runs deep—not just to us, but to generations yet to come.

Terrorism Cannot Be Defeated with War and Violence

The war on terror was based on the faulty premise that terrorism can be defeated militarily. This has been proven false. In fact, since Sept. 11, 2001, the number of worldwide acts of terror per year increased fivefold. Rather than make us safer, the militarized approach to terrorism has opened an endless cycle of retribution and trauma, in which terrorist groups use attacks as their recruiting pitch.

Instead of trying to solve violence with violence, the United States should invest in peace-building strategies that address the underlying drivers of terrorism. This includes engaging in multilateral diplomacy, expanding economic opportunity, and empowering local solutions. These are long-term efforts, to be sure, but are significantly less costly and more sustainable than our current approach.

Congress Must Seize Its Constitutional Authority over War

Shortly after the 9/11 attacks, Congress passed two authorizations—the 2001 and 2002 Authorizations for Use of Military Force, or AUMFs—that gave the president broad authority to wage war across the globe. Thanks to these AUMFs, the war on terror has grown larger and larger with little oversight by Congress.

As a matter of public policy, we believe Congress should exercise its constitutional powers to debate and vote before the president commits our nation to war. Lawmakers have abdicated this responsibility for far too long, and the results have been disastrous for us all.

After two decades of perpetual war, the war-first paradigm is deeply embedded in our government. Uprooting it won't be easy. But frankly, we have little choice. If we truly want our country to be a leader in peace, we must invest in peaceful means to prevent wars and address the underlying harms that lead people to violence.

We can learn the lessons of 20 years of war to prevent future wars.

Hope and Gratitude

FCNL 2021 Annual Meeting » November 20, 2021 » Virtual

Thank you for being present for this event to recognize FCNL's evolution over the last decade and a celebration of my work leading FCNL. My heart is filled with hope and gratitude—to the General Committee, the FCNL staff, our activist network across the country, our generous donors who support this work; and for those who have served FCNL in its 78-year history.

This is an event about all of us—what we have accomplished together and how we are becoming.

If you've read Michelle Obama's memoir entitled, *Becoming*, you'll know what I am talking about. One of the most admired, incredibly successful women in the world writes how she is still "becoming."

She says,

> *"There's a lot I still don't know about America, about life, about what the future might bring. But I do know myself. Your story is what you have, what you will always have. It is something to own."*

Let me tell you a bit of my story. I will also talk about FCNL's story, its evolution, and its becoming. Most of us can point to times in our lives when we thought we should have everything figured out, when we would no longer feel frustrated, unqualified, anxious, or down for not knowing the exact way forward—but the fact is that we are all becoming—as individuals and as an organization.

Our story is written every day by our actions—as we choose hope and work for justice. We are all becoming as we let our lives speak.

Our faith practice of Quakerism is one that teaches us to stay open to continuing revelation. That is how we can experience leadings—both as individuals and as a corporate body.

Here's how I experienced a leading to come to FCNL almost 12 years ago. Several different Friends encouraged me to look at the executive secretary opening at FCNL. I heard them, but I liked my work as executive director of a nonprofit advocating for affordable and supportive housing.

When Friend Ernie Buscemi, whom I did not know at the time but who was on the Search Committee, called to encourage me to become part of the candidate pool, that was a moment that made me listen differently.

Ernie's deliberative, calm invitation to test if this might be a right path for me was the opening that led me to listen inwardly and deepen my discernment. And through the weeks and months that followed, as I spoke with Clerk Gretchen Hall and the search committee, I knew I was held in the Light by them.

I was at ease throughout the process and in making the decision to accept the offer. Without certainty of what relocating to Washington D.C., would mean for my family and what working for FCNL would be like, I knew it represented a new chapter in my becoming. FCNL's vision of the world we seek captured my moral imagination.

When the General Committee approved my appointment at the annual meeting in 2010, it conveyed trust—not only the trust of the General Committee for the search committee's work, but a trust in Divine Guidance.

It is that trust in the movement of the Spirit in our life together that binds us in this gathering—and it is our trust in God's abiding love that allows our comprehension of continuing revelation, our continuing evolution, our becoming.

Evolution means "the gradual development of something, especially from a simple to a more complex form." In fact, in the past decade, FCNL has evolved into a more complex form and we will continue to evolve, continue to become as we live into the possibilities of the beloved community in a society that is racked by violence, inequity, inhumanity, and planetary peril.

FCNL must continue to evolve because the world is more complex. Our comprehension of politics and culture is shaped not only by what FCNL focuses on, but by the constant availability of instantaneous news, information, and entertainment at our fingertips—curated for our individual interests and fed to us by the algorithms of social media platforms.

This competition for attention in a chaotic world challenges us as a Quaker organization committed to practicing integrity and discernment. The ways we communicate and how we choose our affiliations have changed dramatically in the past decade, and especially in the past two years of pandemic time.

FCNL is evolving—we are becoming more diverse—and, in addition to claiming our Quaker identity, we have become more explicit in naming and including people with other identities—through the staff that work at FCNL, through the people who participate in our programs and through our governance.

We claim identity by ethnicity, by race and culture, by religion or no religion, sometimes by Quaker theological background. We claim it by age, by gender, by sexual orientation, by economic and geographic background.

Our vision to seek equity and justice for all and a community in which everyone's potential can be fulfilled is not only for the rest of the world; it's also for FCNL. It is who we are becoming.

To be fully inclusive to all, to fulfill the community agreement we have with one another—we will continue to evolve, shedding some habits and expectations we have of FCNL while holding to the essence of what creates a beloved community.

As Vanessa Julye shared in her teaching yesterday, we must be truthful about our own history as a religious society, acknowledge within our own Quaker meetings our history and discern how we will change. We must be truthful as a Quaker organization—to pursue equity.

There's a lot of history wrapped up into our 78 years together—we celebrate it with joy, and we will acknowledge where we have failed and how we will evolve and continue to grow into the beloved community.

Political realities require us to evolve.

While the 2020 national elections demonstrated an unprecedented turnout for voting, it also revealed a hardcore antipathy to democracy as we have known it and as we imagine what a full democracy could be. The attempted coup to steal the election and the shocking insurrection at the Capitol this year, while directly tied to former President Trump, are not only a phenomenon of the Trump era; rather, they represent a seething white power culture that is alive and dangerous in our country.

How will FCNL evolve to meet the challenge of operating within a governance system that some Americans want to overthrow and other Americans simply do not trust? How do we all live with one another—maybe even our neighbors, whose hateful speech or behavior is alien to our moral grounding to love thy neighbor, no exceptions.

Friends, even as my heart is full of hope and gratitude in being with you and for my decade of service with FCNL, my heart is also broken and tender by the fractures in our society.

My heart is broken that our political leaders have not acted to stop the pain and suffering of millions of human beings across the globe who face violence, poverty, insecurity, and fear and for the very future of our planet as we face the crises that humans have caused and have not yet solved.

Like you, I grieve the loss of over 5 million people from the COVID-19 pandemic across the world—over 750,000 dead in the United States, as well as the suffering and diminished health and wellbeing of millions of people.

The news this week that in one year, this country saw 100,000 deaths from drug overdoses and earlier reports that we are experiencing nearly 50,000 deaths by suicide is further evidence of a society with gaping public health problems, a society that is not putting the welfare of human beings first.

The pandemic has changed us. We are evolving to live with that reality. In this country, the pandemic has demonstrated profound disparities and differences—inequities in employment and healthcare where Black and brown people have experienced greater harm as well as the harsh reality of the angry people whose definition of freedom encourages disregard of public safety for everyone.

We write our story as we move forward. Who FCNL was in 1943, when E. Raymond Wilson began the organization with Friends from yearly meetings across the country, to who we are becoming as we confront today's political and social problems is the story we create together—by choosing hope, acting for justice, and working for peace.

In the past few days, we have written another chapter together in our lobbying for the Build Back Better bill.

When I spoke at this annual meeting 10 years ago after working at FCNL for about eight months, I told the General Committee that we need to be bold, strategic, and relentless in our advocacy for the world we seek.

And we have been—bold, strategic, and relentless.

We Have Been Bold in Building a Bigger, Stronger FCNL

Over the past ten years, our staff size has more than doubled to over 60 positions, and our annual budget has grown to almost $9.5 million this year. We have established new young adult programs, new advocacy and outreach programs that reach across the country and support persistent, relationally driven advocacy.

We have more lobbyists, and we have more legislative priorities. We have more administrative and development support, and we have more real estate on Capitol Hill. We are financially healthy, and we are ambitious in our mission.

While this General Committee governs the organization of the Friends Committee on National Legislation, the companion organizations of the FCNL Education Fund,

Hope and Gratitude

Friends Place on Capitol Hill, and the Quaker Welcome Center are all part of the enterprise.

Our growth in the past decade has been guided by the priorities of the very successful five-year capital campaign from 2012-2017 and by our current Forward Plan, approved by the General Committee in 2017, that has mapped five strategic goals. I would say that there has been an evolution of FCNL—that is, a "gradual development from a simple to a more complex form."

While I have served as executive secretary and now with the title *general secretary* for 10 years, this growth has been possible because of you—this General Committee and those who have served earlier, our current staff and those who have worked at FCNL during the past decade.

I want you to show each other a few of the ways you are involved with FCNL by looking at how you make the FCNL community strong. Most of you in this room belong in one or more of the following categories, or perhaps you have in the past:

» You are a member of an Advocacy Team.

» You participate in any FCNL Young Adult program.

» You are a monthly sustainer.

» You have lobbied with FCNL (that better be 100%!).

» You have stayed at Friends Place on Capitol Hill when it was known as the William Penn House.

» You have written a letter to the editor on one of FCNL's issues.

» You have been involved in any trainings or discussions on how FCNL can become more diverse, equitable, and inclusive.

» You have made a planned gift to FCNL (bequest of charitable gift annuity).

» You have participated in setting legislative priorities in your own Quaker meeting.

» You have encouraged other people you know to advocate with FCNL.

Because of your participation, you have helped make FCNL a bigger and bolder organization with a readiness to take up persistent advocacy on difficult issues—and see problems in a new light.

For example, the Shared Security project that Bridget Moix led with American Friends Service Committee when she was director of Foreign Policy here at FCNL helped us reframe the construct of national security to consider global security and human security as the basis for our advocacy in international policy.

And the project that Diana Ohlbaum has led over the past couple of years of Dismantling Racism/Militarism in U.S. Foreign Policy assesses the patriarchal, racist, and violent foundations of militarism that have undergirded U.S. foreign and domestic policies—at the costs of billions of dollars and millions of lives and livelihood.

Hope and Gratitude

We have been bold in expanding the physical presence of FCNL on Capitol Hill with the creation of the Quaker Welcome Center, an apartment for our Friend in Washington, and now with Friends Place on Capitol Hill— soon to open, welcoming groups to stay in a beautifully renovated guest house in an ideal location just down the street from the U.S. Capitol and a 10-minute walk from FCNL's main office. This program will expand FCNL's vibrant outreach and engagement with young people.

Our legislative priorities—approved by this General Committee—call us to identify, expose, and work to eliminate institutional racism, institutional sexism, and other forms of systemic discrimination in each legislative priority. And in all 12 legislative priorities that you approved in 2020, we work to do just that.

Here are just four of FCNL's legislative priorities:

» Promote nuclear disarmament and non-proliferation,

» Address structural economic inequality,

» Strengthen environmental protections and advance environmental justice,

» Ensure that the U.S. immigration system promotes and respects the rights, safety, humanity, and dignity of all immigrants, refugees, and migrants.

You will revisit these priorities soon as we ask Quaker meetings and churches across the country to offer their discernment and then couple that with our staff's discernment about what FCNL should focus on during the next congressional session. But as you can tell by hearing only four of the 12 priorities, we are bold in laying out an ambitious legislative agenda—even with a larger staff than we had a decade ago—so it is essential for us to be strategic in how we advocate.

We Have Been Strategic in Our Advocacy

We have used the power of our grassroots network—which includes many of you—to bolster the advocacy of our lobbyists on the Hill. The ability of FCNL to show up in so many offices demonstrates our witness and our power.

While we aim to talk to every congressional office on the Hill, there are some states and districts that, because of the member's role on the committee or their willingness to stake out a strong position, become especially important on specific legislation.

Constituents who have relations with members and who are willing to use the relationships for FCNL offer invaluable lift. All our work with congressional offices is richer because of shared constituent and lobbyist interactions.

When the history of repealing the 2002 Authorization for Use of Military Force (AUMF) is written, FCNL will be in that story. Your persistent and strategic focus on the repeal of this outdated statute that, along with the 2001 AUMF, has provided presidential authority without due congressional oversight to wage war and violent conflict, is a vital step toward the world we seek—a world free of war and the threat of war.

This is an achievement worthy of celebration. Full stop. Relish it. Own it. This legislative success, along with the successful approval of the Joint Comprehensive Plan of Action (JCPOA) in 2015, the passage of the First Step Act in 2018, and the Elie Wiesel Genocide and Atrocities Prevention Act in 2019 are huge victories for our lobbying at FCNL.

Of course, our lobbying requires us to be strategic in our communications as well—writing thoughtfully and working to place op-eds; distribute press releases, maintain a vibrant social media presence and a dynamic website; and regularly, although not too frequently, send action alerts, newsletters, and invitations to those who have opted in.

And we are persistently working to get more people to opt in—to join our communications and our advocacy.

We know that our strategic advocacy and these legislative victories would not be possible without persistence. I would say that we are relentless in our lobbying. We are willing to work for many years to achieve these successes, and we are relentless in pressing onward for realizing the full ambition of our goals.

If you are feeling tired, discouraged, or even a sense of despair about the challenges that confront us—and I think we all know these feelings—I encourage you to acknowledge the condition.

If there is one thing I've learned during the isolation of the pandemic, the societal and personal racial reckoning of the past months, and the anxiety from worsening climate catastrophes, it is that taking care of myself means it's OK to step away. It's good to have a support group; it's refreshing to spend time in the natural world; and it's emotionally satisfying to affirm and appreciate one another.

Despite whatever gloom I may experience, I never lose hope, and I encourage you to continue choosing hope. Hope is fundamental. Bryan Stevenson, founder of the Equal Justice Initiative, McArthur Genius awardee, and a hero of mine, calls hope our "superpower." He says,

> *"Don't let anybody or anything make you hopeless. Hope is the enemy of injustice. Hope is what will get you to stand up when people tell you to sit down."*

Faith can also make you stand up and speak up. Our faith comes in many forms—faith in God, faith in our community, faith in the lifeforce that surrounds us. The verse from Hebrews 11 has been a mantra for me during my work at FCNL: "Now faith is the substance of things hoped for, the evidence of things not seen."

I came to work at FCNL because I wanted to lobby for the policies that move our world toward peace, equity, justice, and care of our environment. I have been able to do that with all of you—in times of exciting legislative action and in times of soul-crushing heaviness.

However, during these past 10 years, I have come to understand that FCNL is not only a lobbying organization; we are practicing public theology. As defined by Krista Tippet host of *On Being*, we are "articulating religious and spiritual points of view to challenge and deepen thinking on every side of every important question in public and political life."

That we are a Quaker organization operating from the spirit of love and that we remain open to Divine revelation means that we will never be finished; we will not be able to stop acting for justice and peace and protecting our planet. I hope that FCNL's evolution is always a story of spiritual presence set in this very political environment.

I began by telling you my story of coming to FCNL. The opportunities I have had to travel across the country to Friends meetings and internationally have been rich.

The hospitality I've known in visiting supporters in their homes and understanding their deep commitment to our work that they are able to express with financial support; the excitement and enthusiasm of young adults I've seen as they participate in Spring Lobby Weekend, join our Advocacy Corps, and work as summer interns; and, of course, the growth and development I have witnessed of program assistants who spend a year working with FCNL consistently inspire and give me hope.

I am always impressed by the knowledge, passion, and dedication our staff bring to their work. You know what I'm talking about—you've seen it these last few days. I'm also deeply grateful to our General Committee, especially to the clerks who give so much of their time, spirit, and attention to steward and serve FCNL.

A Closing Story

I want to close my remarks by telling a story that I will always carry with me:

In 2011, shortly after I started working at FCNL, I traveled to Iraq, Palestine, Israel, and Gaza, with a dinner stop in Amaan, Jordan. Jonathan Evans, who worked at FCNL at the time, and who had lived in Jerusalem and taken many groups to visit Israel/Palestine was my travel companion and teacher.

It was both an enchanting and disturbing journey— enchanting to receive the hospitality and warmth of Palestinians who welcomed us in their homes and served us delicious meals and who shared their stories in Amaan, in Ramallah, and in Gaza. We witnessed the aftermath of the fighting of the U.S. war in Iraq while visiting Erbil and Sulaymaniyah.

Through the support of Jim and Debbie Fine, who were working with the Mennonite Central Committee, we saw the witness of Christian Peacemakers and the training of Iraqi seminarians in the Chaldean Catholic Church. It was sobering to be there—to see the destruction and understand the ongoing threats and risks people lived with was to understand that wars don't simply go away when troops pull out.

To cross the Allenby Bridge from Jordan to Palestine was the opening snapshot for me of the Israeli security state. The rich and complex history of place and people is so alive in Jerusalem and throughout the Holy Lands.

Hope and Gratitude

Every person we talked with—whether Israeli or Palestinian—in every neighborhood we visited told us generational stories of oppression and hope.

On the day before we were scheduled to return to the U.S., we gained permission to travel to Gaza. Moving through the heavily militarized check point was reminiscent of entering a prison.

It was a recognition for me of both the isolation and oppression of the 2 million people who live in Gaza, as well as the carceral state we have created in the United States—the mass incarceration and detention measures that lock people away—as if that is an effective solution to problems.

We visited the American Friends Service Committee office in Gaza, a program doing incredible work with youth. We rode by taxi through Gaza, alongside donkey-drawn carts and old vehicles in the dusty streets, seeing crowded conditions, poverty, and the evidence of destruction from the 2008 Operation Cast Lead war.

The contrast of the inequity of Gaza City with Tel Aviv, a vibrant, modern city less than 50 miles away was stark—although not unlike the stark difference in wealth and income inequality we see in U.S. cities.

At the end of that day in Gaza, we were invited to the home of a former colleague of Jonathan, a Palestinian woman and her family whom he had worked with in Jerusalem. Though I was feeling emotionally spent and reluctant to go out, I was blessed by that encounter.

Leading with Hope, Faith, and Love: The Diane E. Randall Collection

It was lovely and restful to be in their home. They shared stories of their lives—the challenge of living under occupation and the joy of their daughter's engagement.

As with everyone we had met on this trip, we asked the question: "What should we tell people in Congress and our colleagues at FCNL about the situation in Iraq or Israel or Palestine?" Many of the answers we'd received throughout the trip were political thoughts, some policy ideas. But, that evening in Gaza, Nazim's comment was to the heart: "Tell them we're human. Tell them we're human beings."

This longing of every soul—to be seen, to be known as a human being—is a truth I think about every day in our work at FCNL. As we are lobbying for an end to U.S. support for the Saudi-led war in Yemen or lobbying for a pathway to citizenship for immigrants or for the tax credit programs to end poverty for families, we are claiming the humanity of every human being, that every human has value. Every human is a beloved child of God.

I firmly believe that as FCNL evolves, as we continue to become, we will remain steadfast in answering to that of God in every human being. FCNL has a unique voice in the cacophony of our current political life. Our peace testimony is not simply an anti-war statement; it is an approach that shuns violence and works to build community globally, nationally, and organizationally.

I believe FCNL's story will always be a story of courage and persistence. But above all, we must remain grounded in the spirit of compassion and speak truth to power. The world, this country, this Congress—indeed every one of us needs one another's commitment to peace; we need our actions for justice.

As we pursue the world we seek—a world free of war and the threat of war, a society with equity and justice for all, communities where every person's potential may be fulfilled, and an earth restored—let us choose hope and abide in love.

Outgoing Clerk Ron Ferguson, outgoing General Secretary Diane Randall, incoming General Secretary Bridget Moix, and incoming Clerk Mary Lou Hatcher. Photo by Cheriss May/FCNL.

About Diane Randall

Diane Randall is the fourth general secretary of the Friends Committee on National Legislation (FCNL) and the first woman in that role. She served FCNL from March 2011 to December 2021.

Diane led FCNL's staff to effectively educate and lobby for the policies and legislative priorities established by FCNL's General Committee. A lifelong advocate for peace and social justice, Diane is a fierce proponent for citizen engagement that advances policies and practices to create a better society for all.

Diane believes that Friends prophetic witness to work for a world that practices peace, equality, community, integrity, and simplicity is often at odds with political life. This effort to pursue truth and to see "that of God in every person we meet" are disciplines that shape FCNL's patient and persistent approach to lobbying for legislation that can help create a more peaceful and just world.

Diane led FCNL's program expansion, including adding lobbyists and new programs to engage grassroots citizens, young adults, and more Quakers to lobby for peace, justice, and a sustainable planet. Diane traveled widely on behalf of FCNL and represented a voice for Quaker advocacy in Washington on Capitol Hill, within the faith community, in media, and throughout the United States.

Before coming to FCNL, Diane was executive director of Partnership for Strong Communities, a Connecticut-based nonprofit organization providing leadership, advocacy, and policy development on solutions to homelessness, affordable housing, and community development.

Diane began her career as a high school English teacher and started working for peace in 1983 as the executive director of the Omaha Nuclear Freeze Campaign.

Diane relocated to Connecticut in 1986, where she directed the state Network to Abolish the Death Penalty and worked for the Office of Urban Affairs of the Archdiocese of Hartford, launching a 20-year career lobbying the state legislature. During that time, Diane became the first executive director of the Connecticut AIDS Residence Coalition.

Diane is a convinced Friend and a member of Hartford Monthly Meeting, New England Yearly Meeting. Diane worships with Langley Hill Friends in Baltimore Yearly Meeting, and she relishes worshiping with Friends across the country while traveling for FCNL.

She serves on the Corporation of Haverford College. Diane previously served on the Sidwell Friends School Board of Trustees, the Board of Advisors of the Earlham School of Religion, the CT Housing Finance Authority Board, the CT Public Defender Services Commission, and the West Hartford Board of Education. She has served on the coordinating committee of the Circle of Protection.

In 2021, the Nuclear Threat Initiative named Diane a Gender Champion in Nuclear Policy in recognition of her role in making FCNL a leading voice for nuclear disarmament and arms reduction. In 2020, Diane was named by the Center for American Progress as one of the 15 "Faith Leaders to Watch" in the United States.

Diane graduated from the University of Nebraska with a B.S. in Education. She is married to Roger Catlin and is the mother of Alex, Lillie, and Nora; she always appreciates spending time with her family.

Diane enjoys walking in Washington, D.C., and in the natural world, reading literature and nonfiction, and cooking from the local farmer's market.

A Minute of Gratitude for Diane Randall

December 2021

We, the Executive Committee of FCNL, on behalf of the General Committee, minute our profound gratitude to Diane Randall for a decade of devotion and visionary stewardship with which she has graced our work. FCNL, as it looks today, reflects the scope of the inspired Forward Plan actualized under her leadership, and it is stronger through the impact of her prophetic work.

Inheriting a strong, well-respected FCNL in 2010, Diane built upon the influence and vibrant programs already in existence by weaving youth advocacy into the national work, embracing a broader Quaker community and fellow travelers, recruiting, and supporting a diverse and professional staff, and widening the circle of sustaining F/friends.

Her faithfulness to the testimonies of equality and integrity gave the work of DEI surety and endurance. With courage, Diane has opened difficult conversations about systemic racism, marginalized people, and injustice wherever it appears. As FCNL has employed a younger, more diverse staff, the Society of Friends has been offered anew the gift of continuing revelation—an opening to change, as we work together in shared communion toward the world we seek.

How does an organization bring its peace-based and spirit-led mission to the unsettled, divided world of Capitol Hill? How can a group respond to both the deep well of internal guidance and the external realities and challenges of politics? And how might an organization which discerns its truths through listening find its voice in the maelstrom of Washington, D.C.? Only by having a leader who is attuned to all these paradoxes, open and balanced, and keeping her eye on the blessed community.

We are grateful to have had such a leader for this past decade. The latter part of that decade presented particularly challenging years of violence, division, attacks on democracy, racial reckoning, global pandemic, and climate disruption. Diane held and inspired the FCNL family with Hope and Faith throughout. She possesses both practicality and moral conviction.

In Diane, FCNL has had a centered and charismatic leader, and, heading into its next years, it is healthy, nimble, sustainable, and faithful to its mission.

Diane Randall joined Circle of Protection faith leaders at the White House in September, 2021 to discuss legislation that could provide historic investments in anti-poverty initiatives and programs to support children and families.